MEMORIES OF THE FERT

BY

JOE WEADICK

Table of Contents

DEDICATION

This book is dedicated to my family as follows:

To my beautiful wife Pat (Sarah Patricia)

Our son Kevin in Australia, his partner Marlies, his daughter Daniela, our grand-daughter, her husband Will
and their daughter Francesca, our great grand-daughter.

Our daughter Ann Margaret in Greece, her husband Manus, our son-in-law. Their daughter Anna Maria, our granddaughter.

Our daughter Debbie in Rathdrum, her husband Davey, our son-in-law, and their two sons Jamie and David.

Our son Joseph, his wife Lynn our daughter-in-law, and their dog Bono.

ACKNOWLEDGMENT

Without the contributions of so many people for which I am truly grateful, this book could not have been written.

1. To Mr. Eddie Howlin, Abbeylands, Arklow, for his contribution of a dangerous incident where the top head flange of the mole pump non return valve in the synthesis plant blew off like a rocket as the nuts on the flange were being slowly loosened. It glanced off the ammonia sphere and landed in the water treatment plant area. Part of the platform steel plates also blew off and were found on top of the cooling tower. It was accepted that the isolation valves on both sides of the non-return valve were closed. The investigation into the incident found that there should not have been pressure in the head flange and it happened due to a design fault.

2. To the four Irish Engineering Co. workers who opened the gate into the fertilizer factory site in 1962 were Seamus O'Brien from Clara Vale. Sean Mc Loughlin from Rathdrum, Tony Hobbs from Gorey and Tim Keogh from Avoca. The first job they had was to erect an embankment around the whole site to protect the factory in the event of flooding. Irish Engineering Co. contracted that work to a Cork company. These four men prepared the site boundary. Three of the men have now passed away. Seamus O'Brien from Clara Vale is still alive and in his late eighties. Seamus was a supervisor in the Civil Department and worked closely with me for a number of years. He retired about one year before we were all dismissed in October 2002.

3. To the co-authors of the book 'The Irish Fertilizer Industry – a history', Mark Cooper and John Davis for giving me permission to write the last three pages of the postscript of their book into my book. I will be ever grateful to them.

4. To Willie O'Loughlin, Manager of the Acid Plants for agreeing to write the Chapter on the Acid Plants.

5. To Donal Keenan, Manager of the Fertilizer Plants, for agreeing to write the Chapter on the CAN Plants.

6. To Joe Weadick, author, for writing the Chapter on the Bagging Loading Plant and the Stacking Area.

7. To Tom Mulhall, Maintenance Foreman, and the author Joe Weadick for writing the Chapter on the Engineering Maintenance Department & Civil Department.

8. To Joe Weadick, Safety Advisor, for writing the Chapter on the Electrical & Instruments Departments.

9. To Damien Nolan, of the Purchasing & Stores Department, for agreeing to write the Chapter on the Purchasing & Stores Departments.

10. To Jack Martin, Personnel Officer, for agreeing to write the Chapter on the Personnel Department.

11. To Danny Hore, Supervisor in the Drawing Office, for agreeing to write the Chapter on the Drawing Office.

12. To Terry Spacey, Manager and Technologist, for agreeing to write the Chapter on the Laboratory.

13. To the author, Joe Weadick, for writing the Preface, Chapter one the Ammonia Plant, Chapter 4 Bagging, loading Plant & Stacking Area, Chapter 5 Welfare, Chapter 6 Security, Chapter 7 Safety and finally The Postscript of the demise of IFI, from the book "The Irish Fertilizer Industry – A History".

14. To Tommy Holden, for giving me valuable information about Bagging & Loading, Pelletizer and the Carbon Plant, all of which plants he worked in.

15. To Sean Grehan, for agreeing to write the chapter on the Roaster Plant.

16. To Pat Fitzgerald for agreeing to write the chapter on CSU & Logistics.

PREFACE

In 1961 the minister for Industry and Commerce set up a state sponsored company, Nitrigin Eireann Teoranta, to erect and operate a nitrogenous fertilizer factory at the location at Shelton Abbey, as stated, near Arklow.

Fuel oil was selected as the main gasification raw material, using the Shell fuel oil gasification process for ammonia production. Consideration was given to the use of pyrites from Avoca Copper Mines for the production of sulphur and sulphuric acid but as the continuing operation of the mines became doubtful because of falling copper prices it was decided to base the initial factory process on imported sulphur. However, the factory was to be so designed as to provide for change-over to Avoca pyrites if supplies from that source were to become economically available at a future date.

CONTRACTORS

The contract for this large chemical complex attracted world-wide interest among chemical plant manufacturers and tenders were invited from leading international contractors from Germany, France, Britain, and U.S.A. The contract went a German consortium headed by Messrs. Lurgi of Frankfurt, associated with Messrs. Uhde of Dortmund, Messrs. Siemens Schuckert of Erlangen, and Messrs. Linde of Munich. This group engaged sub-contractors, principally the Irish Engineering & Harbour Construction Company Ltd., Dublin, for civil engineering work, and Messrs. Wimpy & Company Ltd., London for erection work.

A SERIES OF COMPLEX UNITS

Each of the nine complex units in the fertilizer factory, located in orderly array along the Avoca River, is a vital cog in a wheel which promises to revitalise the land and the soil in Ireland.

The nine units comprise: air separation, ammonia production, sulphuric acid production, ammonium sulphate production, nitric acid production, calcium ammonium nitrate production, phosphoric acid production, compound fertilizer production, and fertilizer bagging and loading.

These units are arranged in what might be called a "critical path" arrangement, each playing a necessary role in the production of fertilizer.

About a third of the factory's electricity is being produced from superfluous steam motivated power and, for the remainder, it is connected to the national grid.

OWN SUPPLY

The factory's own water supply unit supplies cooling water, process water, feed water, and drinking water. After passing through an automatic fine bar screen for removal of mechanical impurities, the water flows to four gravel filters. As the river water is very low in salt and hardness, demineralisation for use as boiler feed water is not necessary.

In the planning of the electrical equipment, the principal considerations were given to constant readiness for operation and the maximum safety of the personnel. In all areas where explosive gas-air mixtures could occur, all electrical equipment, including lighting, and communication system, is of explosion-proof design.

All motors and switchgear are enclosed and most of the switchgear is enclosed in special switch-rooms and not exposed to the influence of harmful or explosive gases.

As an additional safety precaution, this time for foliage in the vicinity of the plant, special care has been taken to ensure that no damage is done to trees by harmful components of the exhaust gases. For this reason the exhaust gases from the sulphuric acid unit are subjected to additional "scrubbing" and the exhaust gases from the nitric acid plant are specially treated before being discharged into the atmosphere. In addition, provisions have been made to ensure that waste waters leaving the factory do not contain any harmful material.

COMPOUND FERTILIZERS.

In the compound fertilizer unit which has a capacity for 100,000 tons per annum, phosphoric acid, mixed with nitric acid is neutralised with ammonia.

A special concentrator developed by Uhde, the German manufacturers of the unit, eliminates the particular problem up to now encountered in other plants of this kind and simplifies the equipment.

The concentrated "mash" is mixed with the required amount of potassium salt and then granulated. After drying, it is coated to prevent caking and stored. The plant off gases are specially treated here also, to keep the atmosphere in the neighbourhood as pure as possible.

It is possible in this unit, by varying the raw material quantities, to produce a great number of different compound fertilizer formulations e.g.: 10:10:20, 6: 12: 18, 15:5:10: etc.

The series of modern, fully automated chemical process plants operate continuously throughout the year, apart from the normal close-down for maintenance.

BENEFIT TO FARMERS

Since Nitrigin Eireann Teoranta came into operation, it is interesting to note that the annual consumption of Nitrogen on Irish farms has increased by more than 80 per cent over a three-year-period. This is all the more remarkable when it is considered the Nitrogen is the only major plant nutrient which does not benefit from Government subsidies to promote its usage. Deserving special mention is the nitrogenous fertilizer calcium ammonium nitrate – sold as "NET NITRATE". Since Nitrigin Eireann commenced production, the demand for calcium ammonium nitrate increased from 30,000 tons to 95,000 tons per annum over a period of three years. Because of such demands, the factory increased its capacity in June 1968 to manufacture 140,000 tons of calcium ammonium nitrate.

The mutual benefits to the farmer, the state, and the industry of increased fertilizer use are indeed substantial. Increased fertilizer use means increased farm output and increased profits to the farmer himself. To the state it means less imports, more exports, and a better balance of payments situation. To the manufacturers it means a more viable industry, more employment, and strong justification for the company's policy of supplying a top-quality product in the right quantity at the right price.

CONCLUSION

A few weeks after the award of the contract in 1962 the extensive earthworks was taken in hand. The Avoca River was trained, and the embankments as a protection against flooding were constructed. Open drains were also constructed leading to a large lagoon at the south east corner of the site. A powerful pump was positioned there for pumping water over the embankment into the river in the event that flooding in the factory became a problem. Most of the buildings and in particular the large fertilizer stores had to be founded on piles.

CHAPTER 1

THE AMMONIA PLANT

Joe Weadick

I was a founding member of the Red Seven Showband, Arklow and started playing on the Irish Showband circuit in January 1960. We were so successful that we changed the name to the Columbia Showband in 1963 and went professional. While the band was still doing well in 1965, I had deep thoughts about my future in the band and decided to leave it and played my last night with them on St Patrick's night in the Entertainment Centre, Arklow. I had married the love of my life Pat Shiel on December 29th 1962 and we had our first child, Kevin, in 1964.

I was aware that the NET fertilizer plant was in the process of starting up so I applied for a job as a cashier because that was what I was working as in Brennan's Bakery and was interviewed in April 1965. I was unsuccessful but the Personnel Manager Patrick Kavanagh asked me if I would be interested in an operator's job and I said 'yes' even though I had no idea what an operators job entailed.

On Sunday May 16th 1965 I was walking up the town going to mass when Mr. Kavanagh told me from across the road to start work the next day May 17th. Needless-to-say I told my wife Pat that I was starting work the next day Monday May 17th and she was delighted.

When I was walking into the Personnel Manager's office on that Monday, I met Mick McGrath who was also starting work that day. I knew that Mick was a bartender in Christie's pub so I gathered that he also had been told by Mr. Kavanagh to start. When Mr. Kavanagh was giving us some information about the factory he showed us some open letters on his desk which were to him from the late Mr. Paudge Brennan, TD from Carnew, giving recommendations for people from Carnew looking for jobs in the factory and told us that this TD wants us to take everyone from Carnew and to forget about Arklow. We believed he was only talking in jest but it did resonate with us.

The man who collected us from the personnel manager's office was no other than Don Laverty - the supervisor on the ammonia plant. I had no idea who he was at the time but I was to work with him for many years on the ammonia plant and such a gentleman he was. On the way down to the site to the ammonia plant I asked him was there any overtime in the job, and he said "in a few months' time you will get more overtime than you want".

Mick, myself, and a number of other operators who had started before us were training on the plant. The person we had most of the time with was another man I had never met but got to know him very well throughout my time on the ammonia plant, that was Dave Brady from Dalkey. I remember very well one day I was sitting on my own in the training room eating my lunchtime sandwiches, feeling down, and Dave came in and asked me how I was getting on with the training and I told him that I was finding it very hard because my previous job, apart from my music career, was a cashier in Brennan's Bakery office. Needless- to-say I was expecting a bit of encouragement but Dave just asked if I was in the wrong job. I never forgot that phrase and reminded him many times over the years … jokingly…

1

During the training the plant process was explained to us and we slowly retained a little at a time. It was explained to us that there will be two operators in the Air Separation plant, three operators on the gasification plant, one in the control room, and two outside on the plant. One operator on the Pellet Boiler, one operator on the pelletizer plant. One operator on 500/600/700 units and 3 operators on 800/900/1000 units and one operator on the water treatment plant.

Mick McGrath and I were delegated to the 500/600/700 units which we were very happy about.

When we were getting close to the plant start-up operator Bill Breslin and I were detailed to put buckets of caustic soda into the top of the open steam drum on the gasification unit for the purpose of flushing and cleaning the inside of the vessel. Neither of us were familiar with caustic soda and we wore our normal overalls and short PVC gloves. As far as I can remember there were no long PVC gloves available on the plant at that time. The shift foreman came to us and said to tie some material around our wrists to protect ourselves.

When I was washing my hands at the end of the shift I realized that my left wrist and the left side of my forehead were black. Bill had similar problems when he washed himself. We both went to the nurse in the First Aid office the following morning. Our burns were dressed and the company doctor was called in to examine us. He confirmed that caustic soda burns were very serious and he told the nurse to continue the treatment on both of us until the burns healed. After a number of weeks when there was no sign of the burns healing the doctor said we will need skin grafts. He made arrangements for us to attend Dr Stevens' Hospital in Dublin. We had our skin grafts and were kept in overnight to ensure we were alright. We were allowed to go home with instructions to have our doctor and nurse keep checking to make sure the skin grafts were healing. It took about two months for the skin graft on my wrist to heal completely but the new piece of skin has been lifeless to this day - 58 years on. That was the only accident I had in my 38 years in the factory, thanks to God.

100 Unit – Air separation Plant

Air from the atmosphere is sucked in through a large air compressor into an air separation unit housed within a massive tank filled with perlite to facilitate the efficient cooling down of the air in order to separate and liquify the O_2(-218 °C and N -210 °C). When they are separated and liquified they are separately brought back up to ambient temperature and piped to an O_2 and N large storage tanks. The tanks are each about 30 ft high and about 20 ft in diameter. They both have a water seal on the bottom.

There are a number of different size valve wheels extended through the large perlite tank from different vessels within the tank for operational reasons.

° The O_2 is taken from the O_2 tank through a O_2 compressor and piped to the gasification plant where it is mixed with steam and into the reactor with heated fuel oil.

The N is taken from the N storage tank, through a N compressor and piped to the 800.

400 Unit Gasification Plant.

The gasification plant has 2 reactors where oil and steam/O_2 mixture enters each reactor at the top and swirls around as the gas goes through and out the bottom through 2 waste heat boilers to cool the crude gas down, into the bottom of the gas scrubber and up through trays where the water coming down washes the carbon out leaving the carbon free gas streaming along to the Purification Plant.

The pressure of the gas stream is controlled at 30 atm. There was one serious incident on the gas line leaving the reactors when the plant was down. A fitter had opened the flange on the line to do some repairs when he got gassed with carbon monoxide. Two of the gasification operators saw him lying on the platform unconscious and they pulled him away from the gas line and revived him.

There is a line to the flare stack coming off the main line before the isolation valve to the Purification Plant. On startup this isolation valve would be closed and the gas stream would be directed up the flare stack until everything is checked on the gasification side and to ensure the units ahead are ready to take the gas. It is important to mention that the last thing done before a reactor is started up is the insertion of the oil gun into the head of the reactor.

The carbon slurry leaves the bottom of the scrubber and enters a slurry tank which is situated at the south side of the plant. The carbon slurry is pumped up 2 levels into a pelletizer plant.

The carbon is mixed with oil in the pelletizers and pellets are produced which are directed via a long chute into the Pellet boiler chamber where it burns to produce high pressure steam.

There was one serious incident on the carbon slurry tank when the top was opened by the operators to check the level and the slurry gushed out of it under pressure and scalded one of the operators.

Beside the slurry tank there was a Sump in case there was need to empty the tank and it was not long before we had to build another sump over the embankment with soil because the original sump was insufficient. On the odd occasion the slurry used to leak into the river so it was decided to build a basin in the field for the slurry on the east side of the factory. This was used for a number of years and it was finally decided to pump the slurry up past Shelton to the mine's tailings.

500 Unit purification Plant.

The gas stream from 400 unit enters the purification tower, goes up through plates and any H_2S in the gas is washed out by a chemical solution coming down through the tower.

600 Unit Converter.

The gas stream goes up through the Saturator vessel through plates with water coming down. The gas leaves the tower at the top. It goes through a large Knock-Out pot which absorbs any water and the dry gas then enters the converter at the top, goes down the inside wall of the converter and up through tubes filled with catalyst. When it comes out of the top of the converter the gas has been converted to H_2 and

3

CO_2. The gas stream then goes up through plates in a large/high Injection Cooler and from there to a water cooler which cools it down to ambient temperature. The converter temperature in controlled at 300 °C.

As the CO_2 in the gas stream is acidic, ammonia liquid is injected via a small pump into the water circulating through the Injection Cooler to control the PH of the water at 7. I believe the PH was not controlled properly and this probably resulted in the erosion of the vessel inside wall causing the subsequent rupture of the Injection Cooler In 1974.

700 unit- CO_2 Removal from the Gas.

The H_2/CO_2 gas goes up through plates in the high Absorption Tower and the water coming down through plates absorbs the CO_2. The H_2 gas then goes through a Knock-Pot where any water still in the gas is removed and the H_2 gas stream is piped to the 800 Unit. There is a line to the flare stack from this gas line before the isolation valve. On plant startup the gas will be sent to the flare stack first until the 800 unit is ready to take it. As before the gas pressure is controlled at 30atu.

The CO_2 saturated water from the bottom of the absorption tower and the knock-out pot goes into the large concrete sump (approx. 15ft square and 15ft high) and air is blown up through large wooden trays in the very high (about 100 ft high) degassing tower by 2 large fans situated on the top of the concrete sump and the CO_2 is blown up and out the vent on the top of the tower.

The H_2 gas and N gas joins together (1- H_2 + 3-N) and goes through the 1st & 2 stages of the synthesis compressor where it is pressurized to about 100 ats. It leaves there and goes up through the plates in the copper liqueur tower where any traces of CO and H_2S are removed. The gas then goes through the 3rd and 4th stages of the compressor where it is pressured up to 470 ats. It then goes through the separator, injector, and into the converter. It leaves the bottom of the converter and goes through the waste heat boiler, water cooler, separator, expansion vessel and into the ammonia sphere. Any gas not converted to ammonia circulates through the mole pump and back into the converter.

Plant Cooling Water System.

A cooling water tower about 80 ft long/20 ft wide/30 ft high has 2 large pumps which pumps the water through all water coolers on the plant and returns entering the tower on the top. The water is cooled as it falls down through wooden lats and from the air blowing up from about 10 large air fans on the top.

Water Treatment Plant

The water treatment plant is situated between the 700 unit and the ammonia sphere and consists of 8 vessels containing gravel sitting on a steel plate with holes in it to allow the water flow through and out the bottom of the vessel into a main pipeline which serves the whole factory. There are also 3 smaller vessels beside the filters in which the water is softened for use in the steam making units.

There is a large underground pipe bringing water in from the river to a sump just inside the embankment and there are 4 pumps which pump the river water to the filters. There is one operator manning this plant and he backwashes each filter as required. He also looks after all the pumps and calls the shift foreman if there is a problem. There is a small office near the filters where the operator looks after the PH meters and soft water meters. When the incident happened on the 600 unit, he took to the river bank for his own safety.

New Water Treatment Plant (built about 1972)

The new water Treatment Plant was built on the north east side of the cooling tower. It was completely different to the first plant. It was circular and was about 40 ft. in diameter on the top and about 5 ft diameter at the bottom.

Water was brought in from the river under the embankment, into a sump near the tailings pond. There were three sump pumps and they pumped the river water over and into the bottom of the treatment plant. There was a scheduled amount of mineral water pumped into the treatment plant from the shed which contained three tanks, each holding water and chemical mixture. A scheduled amount from each tank was pumped into the treatment tank to form a blanket at about the middle of the tank. The river water entering from the bottom rose up through the blanket and was clean and at 7.0 P.H. The treated water left the tank from the top and was pumped up the site to all plants as required by three large pumps.

On the commissioning of this new plant the water treatment operator, when asked, told his foreman that he was not allowed to operate the plant by his shop steward. It resulted in a strike by the operators throughout the factory and lasted three weeks before it was resolved.

Ammonia SPHERE No. 2.

This sphere was built east of the new water treatment plant in 1979 to increase storage capacity in preparation for Marino Point coming on line.

Factory Oil Tank

There is a 50 ton oil tank on the south side of the cooling tower which serves the factory. Heavy fuel oil is imported by ship into Arklow Harbor and transferred to the factory oil tank in a steam traced pipe. There is a steam heater where the oil enters the tank and the temperature is controlled at about 80 deg's. There are 3 pumps adjacent to the pipe track which pumps the oil to the 400 Unit reactors, the pellet boiler and the pelletizer. Oil can also be pumped up to the A & F plants as required.

Propane Storage Tanks.

There are 2x10 ton propane storage tanks situated near the oil storage tank for use on the top of the flare stack. It is important that the flare stack is always lighting.

CO_2 Plant

The first of two CO_2 plants was built in 1971. It was situated on the south side of the 700 unit. The CO_2 gas was piped down from the top of the degassing tower into the bottom of a permanganate vessel to remove any impurities. The gas comes out the top of the permanganate vessel, through carbon filters and through the bottom of another vessel to dry the CO_2 and out the top of the vessel and into a compressor where it is pressurized to about 20 ats. From there it goes to a refrigeration system where it is liquified. The liquid CO_2 is then piped up to one of two 50-ton storage tanks which are situated on the west side of the Air Separation Plant.

The Dry Ice Plant was built adjacent to the storage tanks. To make dry ice the liquid CO_2 is pumped into the dry ice building where there are two dry ice making machines. The liquid CO_2 is compressed in one of the machines until it is a block of dry ice. The machine is then shut down and depressurized. Then the door is opened and the block of dry ice comes out on a small conveyer. The operator then puts the dry ice cube into a wrapper and puts it into a special insulated box which holds about a ton of dry ice. The dry ice is sold to various companies.

A second larger CO_2 plant was built in 1973 on the north side of the synthesis compressor building with a 200 Ton liquid CO_2 storage tank. These CO_2 plants operated until the ammonia plant was shut down in 1981.

Carbon Plant NET-KETJIN built in 1971

Because the carbon from our gasification plant was regarded to be of very good quality for use in batteries, music records, and a number of other technical uses it was decided to build a carbon plant in conjunction the Ketjin company.

Large bags of carbon slurry were brought to the carbon plant from the carbon tip-head and one by one they would be processed into dry carbon pellets, bagged in 25 kilo paper bags. Twenty of these bags would be put on pallets. Each pallet would be shrink-wrapped and stored for sale.

If I remember correctly, the carbon arriving in the large approximately one-ton weight bags, would contain about 90% water. The carbon would be poured into a drum where it would be processed until most of the water was removed. The carbon would then go through a toluene liquid tower to remove any impurities. From the toluene vessel the almost pure carbon would be piped into a long drier. Coming out the exit tube from the drier the carbon would be completely dry and have the appearance of carbon pellets. It then would be blown up to a dry carbon silo in the bagging shed by a powerful fan.

The bagging plant operator would place and secure a brown bag under the chute on the bagging platform and open the top slide valve. 25 kilos of dry carbon would drop down into the box. The operator would then close the top slide valve and open the bottom slide valve and the 25 kilos of carbon would drop down into the bag. The operator would then securely close the bag and place it on a wooden pallet. When 20 bags were put on the pallet it would be shrink-wrapped and stored for sale.

It was recognised by management that the Carbon Plant (particularly the bagging plant) working conditions were so dirty that all carbon plant operators got all their work clothes including their underwear free and 12 bars of soap daily because they would get so dirty during their shift that they would need a shower and plenty of soap to get all the carbon off their bodies before transferring into their private clothes to go home. There was a large washing machine and drier which was manned by a welfare operator to ensure the carbon plant operators were properly looked after.

After about five years using carbon from the 400 unit, it was decided to import a better-quality carbon from Holland.

The carbon plant was manned by 2 operators on the plant and 2 operators in the bagging shed.

SIX DANGEROUS INCIDENTS ON THE AMMONIA PLANT DURING ITS LIFETIME

1. Injection Cooler

There was an explosion one night at about 01.00 hrs. The lights went out on the whole factory and the town of Arklow. I was looking at television at home and I knew by instinct that it must be the factory so I jumped in my car and drove out right away. I spoke to the security man at the gate and he told me there was an explosion on the ammonia plant. I drove down to the plant and the Arklow Fire Brigade had just arrived and were parked on the road behind the plant control room. I realized that all the windows in the control room had been blown out with the vacuum in the air as a result of the rupture. Most of the windows were also blown out on the east side of the Air Separation compressor house and the west side of the synthesis compressor house. The two operators in the control room had laid down on the floor to protect themselves. The shift foreman on that night, my friend Mick O'Toole, was in the control room when the rupture happened and he said that stones and pieces of glass penetrated the windows and peppered the panel causing damage to the instruments before the windows were sucked out.

Mick went looking for the operators and found most of them in the maintenance workshop. He would not let the electrician put on the lights because there was water leaking all over the plant.

The top half of the vessel blew upwards like a rocket, over the pipe track and landed on the stairs up to the top of the ammonia sphere breaking off some of the steel supports and damaged one of the sphere legs. We were very fortunate that it did not pierce the sphere. If it had, Arklow town would have suffered severely from the effects of the leaking ammonia.

The bottom section of the vessel shifted and caused a lot of damage in the area of the vessel including fracturing the water lines in and out of the injection cooler, gas lines and platform steel plates. There was also a fire in the bottom of the injection cooler immediately after the rupture. It did not last long, possibly some hydrogen gas.

Mick and I put on breathing apparatus and spent 2 hours closing valves throughout the plant and making it as safe as possible. The firemen supplied us with air bottles for our breathing apparatus.

Mick McGrath, another of my fellow foremen, arrived in at 2 a.m. when he heard about the Injection Cooler rupture. He examined the devastation caused by the rupture on the 600 unit and the damage at the sphere.

Mick told me that the operators working in the control room that night were Larry Duffy on the 400 Unit control panel, Barney Christy on the synthesis panel, and Tommy Dillon on the 800 Unit compressors.

There were two major investigations carried out. One by NET Management and the other by ICI. They both came to the same conclusion. Low PH in the Injection Cooler for many years resulting in erosion of the inside walls of the injection Cooler until it ruptured. A new Injection Cooler had to be made in Germany. The plant was down for over three months as a result of the Incident.

2. 600 Unit knock-out pot failure

The bottom broke off the knock-out pot after the saturator on 600 unit with a massive bang and it blew a large hole in the ground underneath it. Stones from the ground flew all over the place. We were fortunate nobody was in the immediate area so there were no injuries. All the windows blew out of the water treatment office and the operator took to the river bank for his own safety. Engineering Department carried out an investigation and found that it was a design problem.

3. 400 unit – O_2 in Reactor

An incident occurred where O_2 got into a reactor before the oil was introduced resulting in the O_2 going through the whole system causing an implosion in the gasification scrubber collapsing all the trays and it went up the flare stack and blew a large hole near the top.

My memory of this incident is that originally there was only one O_2 block valve and when this incident occurred a second isolation valve with a bleed valve was fitted between the two valves which had to be checked before oil was introduced. It was accepted that starting up gasification reactors is one of the most dangerous jobs on the ammonia plant.

4. 1000 Unit

The top flange on the mole pump circulation system non-return valve blew off like a rocket when maintenance personnel were loosening the bolts on it. The isolation valves before and after the valve were closed and there should not have been any pressure there. It glanced off the sphere and landed somewhere near the river. Some sections of the platform flew off also and were found on the top of the cooling tower. The incident was investigated and it was found that there was a fault in the design of the head flange.

5. O_2 & Nitrogen Storage Tanks

An incident occurred once during an annual shutdown where the complete top of one of the storage tanks flattened. It would appear that there was a vacuum created in the tank for some reason.

6. A large red-hot bulge was noticed during a normal check by an operator on the reactors in 400 Unit gasification plant one night. This was serious so the reactor in question was shut down immediately. When the temperature of the reactor cooled down sufficiently to remove the head, it was taken off and an investigation took place to see what caused the hot bulge. It was agreed that the problem

8

was that some of the carborundum bricks in the reactor were starting to break down. Had we not closed the reactor down immediately it could have exploded resulting in a lot of collateral damage, not to talk about what injuries could have been caused to workers in the immediate area.

The reactor was down for about one month to have the bricks removed and replaced by new carborundum bricks. Before the reactor was put back on line it had to be heated up to normal working temperature and kept at that temperature for three days to ensure it would not result in the same problem when put on line again.

AMMONIA PLANT FUNCTION IN 1974

A function was organized by the Ammonia Plant staff in the Arklow Bay Hotel in 1974 and my wife Pat and I attended it without knowing why it was being held.

I only realized the reason for it when I was called up to the stage and presented with six Waterford cut glasses from our Ammonia Plant Manager Alan Fewster on my departure from the Ammonia Plant to take up my new role as the Factory Welfare Officer. My wife Pat was presented with a bouquet of Flowers. Then our Ammonia Plant supervisor Don Laverty was called up and presented with six Waterford cut glasses on his departure from the plant to take up the role of Plant Superintendent in the Roaster Plant. Don's wife was also presented with a bouquet of flowers.

It was something neither I nor Don ever expected but we were delighted with the gesture from our Ammonia Plant colleagues and will never forget. Nothing like that ever happened again and I can only say thank you to all our Ammonia Plant colleagues and our Plant Manager Alan Fewster.

CHAPTER 2

THE ACID PLANTS

Willie O'loughlin

THE SULPHURIC ACID UNIT

The sulfuric acid unit operates by the classical contact process. The starting materials are elementary sulphur and hydrogen sulphide gas from sulfinol wash. The unit produces 212 tons per day of sulfuric acid of 98% strength, and high pressure steam (40 atm.). It can also handle gases from the roasting of Avoca pyrites, should this become necessary in the future. By neutralisation with ammonia the waste gases from the sulphuric acid unit are practically free of sulphuric dioxide. The ammonium sulphate obtained in the process is likewise utilised for the production of fertilizers. The neutralisation of the waste gas in conjunction with H_2S combustion ensures that air pollution in the Avoca Valley is kept at a minimum.

The elementary sulphur is melted and burnt in a furnace. Part of the heat of combustion is utilised for the production of high-pressure steam (40 atm. 400 C°) in a subsequent waste heat boiler, this steam being fed to a condensation turbine. The sulphur dioxide formed is converted to sulphur trioxide in the converter in the presence of vanadium pentoxide-containing catalyst. The heat of reaction is used to preheat the process air in external heat exchangers. The SO^3 gas leaving the converter, after cooling the heat exchanger with process air, passes to the absorption tower where it is absorbed by circulating sulphuric acid. The liberated heat of absorption heats up the sulphuric acid and is eliminated via cooler in the acid circulation system.

The gas leaving the absorption tower is washed in a neutralization tower with ammonium sulphite-bisulphite solution which absorbs the SO_2 gas. The concentrated wash liquid is discharged and treated with sulphuric acid, whereby ammonium sulphate solution and SO_2 gas is formed. The solution is stripped with air, and the SO_2 thus separated is returned to the sulphuric acid unit. The SO_2-free ammonium sulphate solution is pumped to the fertilizer plant.

The hydrogen sulphide from Sulfinol wash is burnt with air in a furnace to form sulphur dioxide. Part of the heat of combustion is eliminated from the gas in a subsequent radiation cooler. The gas is then sprayed with diluted sulphuric acid in a venturi scrubber and cooled. The resulting mist is separated in a ceramic filter. The filtered SO_2-gas is finally passed to the drying tower.

"In June 1972 myself, Pedro Travers, Peter Doyle and Leslie Sargent started training in the Nitric Acid Plants 1300 and 2300 in preparation for the commissioning and start up of the new 4300 which was being built across the road from the existing plants. The control room for the new plant was located in13.2300 control room. At that time the existing crew were

Team 1. Michael Byrne (manager) John O'Sullivan

Team 2. Tom Byrne (sting) Michael Halpin

Team 3. Finton O'Connor, Ned Dempsey

Team 4.Christy O'Connor, Mick Hughes (mate)

Training for the Acid Plants was initially on days in Adm. 2 in Sean Walsh's office where we had to learn the Process Flows and P&I Drawings. We would be sent up to the plant in the afternoons to follow and identify lines and instrumentation. We would also get to meet the different Shift teams. After approximately two months we were put on shift and I was on Team 2 with Tom Byrne senior operator and Michael Halpin junior operator.

At the back of the 13/2300 plants were three Nitric Acid storage tanks and a pumping system to supply the 1400 can plant and the C.C.F. Plant. Located behind the storage tanks was the acid carboy filling station which was operated by the Harbour Operators. There was also a facility for loading acid tankers for sales and also for transferring acid to a storage tank at the harbour. Michael O'Brien was the foreman over this area.

Located on the ground floor of the 1300 Plant was a 40/20 steam pressure reducing system which was controlled by the Nitric Acid Plants and also alongside the 1300 was a large Cooling Tower and the acid plants were responsible for the supply of cooling water to the 1400 and C.C.F. Plant. The water treatment for this system and also the 2300 cooling system were the responsibility of the Nitric Acid Operators. Working in the Nitric Acid Plants at this time was very rewarding because apart from the actual operation of the plant itself we were an integral part of the whole site plant network. We had a detailed knowledge of the site steam system as users when we were starting up plants and as exporters when the plant was on line.

The process flow for the Nitric Acid Plants in simple terms consisted of passing a filtered flow of air and ammonia in a measured ratio of 10% across a platinum/Rhodium Gauze at a temperature of 880°C. This chemical reaction converted the air/ammonia mixture to Nitrous Oxide and the heat of reaction was used to generate steam which was used internally to run the turbine and any excess was exported to the factory steam network. The Nitric oxide was then passed through an absorption system where secondary air was added to the process and process water was pumped into the system to end up with Nitric Acid of 56%. Because of the huge cost of the Platinum/Rhodium gauzes, underneath these gauzes was a recovery gauze consisting of Gold/Palladium to trap the Platinum that might fall through. The cost of this pack was several hundred thousand pounds for the smaller plants alone and eventually when Nitric Acid 5 came along the cost of the whole pack was close to half a million. At this time the gauzes were collected at Dublin Airport accompanied by a garda and on occasion if the gauzes were delivered the night before the garda would be present in the control room overnight.

The Gauze changing would take place initially on the smaller plants every sixteen weeks and the plant would be a hive of activity to get the burner opened up and gauzes changed out and the plant ready for start-up in a twelve-hour shutdown window. Other maintenance work would be carried out also. Pascal Foley was the maintenance foreman at this time.

The Nitric Acid Plants at the time were under the same supervision as 1400 Can plant and the foremen over the area were, Donal Keenan, John Roche, Peter Kearns, Brendan Bowler and Frank Brennan. The supervisor at the time was

Sean Walsh and the plant Superintendent was Jim Killeen. Barney Ryan and Alan Grimes were also involved in Technical Support and training.

Following the successful start-up and commissioning of 4300 Unit, the next expansion of the Nitric Acid Plants was the building of the 3600 a couple of years later. This plant was built alongside the 4300 and a new control room was built in this plant for to monitor both the 4300 and the 3600 plants although the 4300 panel was not transferred over from the 13/2300 side until the 3600 had been commissioned. The new control room also had a safe built in to store the replacement gauze packs for the four plants. This plant was built to cater for the increased demand for Nitric Acid with building of the 2400 Priller Can Plant.

The manning of the new acid plant increased the crew by another four people and myself. Brendan Kincaid, Mick Hughes and Pat Power were promoted to Senior Operators and Tom Hynes, Sean Kelty, Mick Thewlis and Joe Ivory had joined the team.

The acid plants at this time were under the C.C.F. Supervision and the foremen were Tom Halpin, Sean Maguire, Tony Domoney, Jim Elliott and Mick Byrne. Dave Brady was the supervisor and Andy Cusack was the plant manager.

As the newer plants came along the basic process remained the same but there was huge advancements in instrumentation and energy saving techniques. The efficiency of the process increased significantly with the higher pressures the absorption systems were operated at. This reduced the Tail Gas content going to atmosphere from the stack. In the case of the 3600 plant the stack gas was clear and this was a huge breakthrough from the Environment impact. The most significant change with the 3600 was the fact that there was only a single absorption tower compared to the two towers in the first three plants. Some time later an additional electric driven air compressor was built to boost the plant load on the 3600. This was known as the Joy Compressor.

During this time there were a number of personnel changes due to redundancies, closure of C.C.F. and rationalisation around the site. Jody Hughes and Denis Hannigan came from the C.C.F. Plant and Paul Redmond, John Kavanagh and Eddie Mc Elheron were there also. At this time Pat Ryan was Technical Manager and Jim Fanning Electrical Engineer.

The fifth and final Nitric Acid Plant to be built was NA 5 and this was a game changer from the point of view of acid production and steam generation. The Plant had been in operation in Scotland and was an I.C.I. plant. It had been decommissioned and the plant was dismantled and transported to Arklow. The logistics of transporting the plant and in particular the absorption tower from Arklow harbour to the site was a major feat in itself and involved the closure of Templerainey roads, dismantling of power lines, widening of roads in some areas to bring the tower to site on a specialised transporter.

The N.A. 5 Plant was successfully erected and commissioned and as a result the original 13/2300 were closed and decommissioned, and sometime later the 4300 was shut down and decommissioned also. The N.A. 5 plant was able to export enough steam to run the whole site without having to burn any oil.

A gas fired 17atm. Boiler was built in the 4300 plant to supply steam for N.A. plant start-ups, however no boilers were required when NA 5 was running.

At this time the site was very rationalised with two acid plants and two Can plants. The new Can plant then replaced the Priller.

Niamh Healy had come on board as Environmental and Technical Engineer during the NA 5 commissioning and Rochella Mulvihill replaced her in the same role."

During the lifetime of the factory there were 5 nitric acid plants built. The process was the same but the volume of each plant differed. I now will explain the process.

Nitric acid is manufactured By the Uhde process in three stages:

1. Oxidation of ammonia to form nitric oxide.

2. Oxidation of nitric oxide to form nitrogen dioxide.

3. Absorption of nitrogen dioxide in water to form nitric acid.

The first stage is the oxidation (i.e. combustion) of ammonia in air. The ammonia should react with oxygen in the air on a catalyst of platinum – rhodium gauzes to form nitric oxide. The reaction is as follows:

$$4 NH_3 + 5 O_2 = 4 NO + 6 H_2O$$

Ammonia will also react with oxygen to form nitrogen and water as follows:

$$4 NH_3 + 3 O_2 = 2N_2 + 6H_2O$$

This ammonia is wasted. The combustion must be controlled to ensure that the first reaction predominates.

This is done by:

1. Using the specified platinum – rhodium catalyst.

2. Using absolutely pure ammonia and air.

3. Controlling the combustion temperature between 880° and 890° C

In practice 95 to 96% of the ammonia is converted to nitric oxide. The remainder is wasted.

The second stage is the oxidation of nitric oxide to form nitrogen dioxide. The nitric oxide reacts with oxygen remaining in the air after the ammonia combustion as follows:

$$2\ NO + O_2 = 2NO_2$$

The reaction occurs as the gases pass from the burner through the boiler and heat exchangers to the cooler condenser. By the time the gases reach the cooler condenser about half the nitric oxide has been converted to nitrogen dioxide.

In the cooler condenser the water which was formed in the ammonia combustion condenses and absorbs virtually all the nitrogen dioxide which has been formed up to that point.

$$3NO_2 + H_2O = 2HNO3 + NO$$

Because there is more water than there is nitrogen dioxide, the acid formed here is weak (about 35%) . It is pumped into the absorption tower at the point where the acid is at the same concentration.

It can be seen that more nitric oxide is formed by the absorption – one ton for every three tons of nitrogen dioxide absorbed. Nitric oxide cannot be absorbed. It must be converted to nitrogen dioxide before it can be. Extra oxygen is provided by the introduction of secondary air after the gas cooler. The remaining nitric oxide is then converted to nitrogen dioxide. This occurs in the bottom of the primary tower.

The Nitrogen dioxide is then absorbed in water to form nitric acid. As before some nitric oxide is formed in the absorption – one ton for every 3 tons of nitrogen dioxide absorbed.

As the gases pass through the towers, the oxidation of nitric oxide and the absorption of nitrogen dioxide to form nitric acid and a smaller amount of nitric oxide is repeated. It is vital to have sufficient oxygen remaining in the gas for the successive oxidations.

The gas leaving the top of the secondary tower should therefore contain at least 3% oxygen.

The absorption efficiency is normally 98.5 to 99%. The amount of water used is controlled to give a product acid strength of 55 to 58%.

Both the oxidation and absorption reactions are more efficient the lower the temperature and the higher the pressure. The gas temperature at the inlet to the primary tower should not exceed 50 C.

Each of the three reactions in the nitric acid process gives out considerable amounts of heat. With the specified ratio of ammonia to air in the burner the heat released by the combustion of ammonia maintains the burner temperature at 880 to 890°C. Wastage of ammonia is then minimised. The heat is recovered in the waste heat boiler to generate steam and the steam turbine drives the air compressor.

The heat released by the oxidation and absorption reactions should be removed quickly – both reactions are more efficient the lower the temperature. Otherwise, the temperature of the gas will rise and the efficiency of the reactions will drop off. This would reduce the overall efficiency of the process and give a bad stack. The heat is removed in the various coolers and by the cooling coils in the absorption towers. It is vital that cooling water tubes are kept clean. Consequently, very tight control of cooling water conditions is necessary.

Nitric Acid No. 1 went on line in July 1965

Nitric Acid No.2 went on line in July 1965

Nitric Acid No. 3 went on line in 1972?

Nirtic Acid No. 4 went on line in 1975?

Nitric Acid No. 5 went on line in 1993?

PHOSPHORIC ACID UNIT

Since NET wants to produce, besides nitrogenous fertilizers, also NPK fertilizers, it was decided to extend the factory by the incorporation of a phosphoric acid plant and a compound fertiliser plant.

The phosphoric acid unit is supplied by the firm of Friedrich Uhde and operates by the process of "Nissan Chemical Industries". It produces phosphoric acid of approximately 30-32% P_2O5 from rock phosphate and sulphuric acid. In this process the phosphate is decomposed at a temperature of approximately 95° C by sulphuric Acid, the calcium formed by the reaction being a semi-hydrate.

The reaction mash is cooled in a series of crystallizers to approximately 50° C, whereby the semi-hydrate is converted into large, regular-shaped, easily washable dehydrate crystals.

The phosphoric acid is separated from the gypsum on a continuous belt filter. After passing through two washing steps the gypsum can be used without further purification for the production of gypsum slabs. It can also be employed as raw material for the production of ammonium sulphate or in the cement industry.

CHAPTER 3

THE FERTILIZER PLANTS

AMMONIUM SULPHATE UNIT

In this unit gaseous ammonia and sulphuric acid are admitted to the saturator, where concentrated ammonium sulphate solution is formed. In the course of the process ammonium sulphate crystals are precipitated. By means of vibration centrifuges, the latest development in this field, crystals are separated from the mother liquor. The crystals are treated in a drying cooler until a final humidity of 0.1% is achieved. The air enriched with ammonium sulphate dust leaving the drying cooler is purified in a wet dust separator. The resulting ammonium sulphate dust and water mixture is recycled in the saturators. Moreover, ammonia water from ammonia synthesis and ammonium sulphate solution from sulphuric acid production are processed in the saturators. By the addition of chemicals ammonium sulphate in the form of course crystals strewing properties is produced.

CALCIUM AMMONIUM NITRATE PLANT

The plant produces 200 tons per day of ANL with 20.5 to 27.5% nitrogen and comprises the following sections:

A. Limestone Grinding Section

The limestone (dolomite) containing approximately 17% MgO for the production of ANL is supplied in lorries and ground in an air flue grinding unit to the required fineness and dried at the same time. The ground limestone enters the production section with a final humidity of about 0.15 to 0.2%

B. Neutralisation and Concentration of Ammonium Nitrate

The liquid ammonia is evaporated whereby chilled air for product cooling is produced. Gaseous ammonia and nitric acid with about 55% HNO_3 are converted to ammonium nitrate solution, the solution being largely concentrated by utilising the reaction heat. Final concentration is affected in concentrators heated with steam saturated at 7 atm. The vapours are condensed in surface condensers. Most of the vapour condensate is re-used as process water in the nitric acid unit, so that nitrogen losses are only small.

C. ANL Granulation Section

The limestone powder with the ammonium nitrate solution is granulated in a screw conveyor by the improved UHDE process. Although the granulation of dolomite is particularly difficult, the granules produced have a very nice spherical shape and a final humidity approx..0.4to 0.5. The grain size can be varied within a wide range e.g. 80-90% may be within the size range of 2-4 mm. When required, a size range of between 1.5 and 3 mm may also be produced by suitably adjusting the granulating equipment. The calcium nitrate content of the product can be kept very low by applying especially short residence times.

The ammonium nitrate limestone produced by the UHDE process is stable and does not require the addition of inhibitors.

<u>CAN1</u>

CAN 1 was the first CAN granulation plant to be brought into production in the Republic of Ireland. It was designed by the German company Fredrich Uhde GMPH from Dortmond. The plant had a design capacity of 200 tonnes per day of 20.5% Nitrogen. Over the 38 years of its operation the capacity had been in increased to 465 tonnes per day of 27.5% Nitrogen. This product was marketed as NET Nitrate. The increases in the plant capacity was achieved by a number of methods. Engineering, use of new technology, new and more efficient operating methods and the introduction of computerised control.

In a Granulation Plant there are three main Operating systems. Production and control of Ammonium Nitrate, Conditioning of the product and production of Limestone (Dolomite) of a suitable size.

Production and Control of Ammonium Nitrate.

Liquid Ammonia is vapourised and dried and added to a vessel called a Neutraliser where Nitric Acid is added under ratio control to produce Ammonium Nitrate at an alkaline PH to ensure stability. The Neutralising column was packed with stainless rashig rings and ceramic saddles of 50mm diameter. The Ammonium Nitrate produced in the Neutraliser was 78.0%. This was then concentrated in two stages using heat from 7 bar steam and under vacuum in a series of heat exchangers. The concentration of the Ammonium Nitrate required was 97% at a temperature of 155°C.

Limestone (Dolomite) from Kilkenny was delivered by trucks, at a maximum size of 50mm. This was crushed in a series of Ball Mills and dried to powder of a maximum size of 500 microns in diameter, at least 60% of this powder was less than 64 microns.

The next stage of the process was to pump the 97% Ammonium Nitrate at a controlled rate to a Pugmill granulator where it was mixed with a controlled flow of Limestone and recycled CAN. This recycle was made up of undersized and oversized product from screening and crushing. Granulation was controlled at temperatures between 108°C and 113°C. The granules formation was completed in a rotary Dryer, from where they screened and then cooled to less than 32°C and conveyed to the bulk stores. Drying of the product was by oil fired furnace, this was eventually replaced by using a waste steam heater eliminating the use of fossil fuel. Product transported to the bulk storage had a size specification of 90% between 2mm and 4mm diameter.

<u>CAN 2</u>

In 1972 the then Company Chairman announced that the board of Directors had approved a proposal to increase the production of CAN to meet the increased demand for fertiliser by the Agricultural sector in Ireland.

This new facility was a CAN Prilling Plant and was a French design (S.T.E.C) and it required the Ammonium Nitrate to be concentrated to 99.8% at a temperature of 180°C, to achieve these parameters 14 bar steam was used in the final evaporation system. The temperature of the Ammonium was strictly controlled at 180°C, and pumped to a homogeniser placed on the top of a 47-meter concrete tower. The homogeniser contained an agitator to mix the Ammonium Nitrate, recycled CAN from the screening and crushing systems, and Dolomite pneumatically transferred from the Milling system. The resultant mix was sprayed through a series of plates containing from 995 to 1155 holes.

The product was called Prills and they were collected on a 2-meter-wide conveyer belt at the base of the tower, transferred to the screening systems and then to Fluid Bed Coolers and after anti caking treatment was applied transferred to bulk storage. Fines and off specification product were returned pneumatically to the Homogeniser for remelting. The cooling and solidifying of the Prills spraying down the Prill tower was accelerated by the use of four large fans situated on the top of the tower to draw air up through the falling stream.

CAN 3

In the 1990's as farming methods were changing very much. New spreading machines were being designed for the agricultural sector, farmers continued to try and reduce costs and labour times to spread fertilisers. Prills had a smaller mean size than granules and therefore could not spread as wide an angle, so they required more passes in a field using more fuel and time. Complying with new environmental standards was introducing excessive cost in Prill production and could not be sustained. The UHDE technology used in CAN 1 among others was researched and found to fill all the requirements to meet the objectives. CAN 3, a granulation plant was purchased and constructed on the site of the now defuncted Ammonium Sulphate plant.

Can3 required Ammonium Nitrate at 97% thus the final evaporation system was taken out of service in CAN 2 reducing the safety of handling Ammonium Nitrate. The neutralising section in CAN 2 was still required by CAN 3. The control systems for CAN 1 and Can 3 were amalgamated and computerised in a new central control room. The Pugmill granulator was basically similar to the original type in use in CAN 1 from 1965, however it had remote speed adjustment. The flows of Dolomite and Ammonium were controlled by Coriolis measuring devices which were very reliable and accurate.

The drying of the product in the Dryer was carried out by autothermal means using the air from the Fluid Bed cooler. The dust from the Dryer cyclones was regulated by plastic dust locks, an invention by a young engineer named Nebel in a sugar making facility in Holland. Another major addition to CAN 3 was the installation of a scrubbing system collecting all dust and gasses that could be returned and reused in the process, this system had the capacity and was used to collect and also used the similar streams from CAN 1.CAN 3 was also used to produce a product with 5% sulphur called Super Net. This product was produced by replacing the Dolomite with Gypsum from Gypsum Industries in Cavan.

Over the years there were numerous rationalising programmes implemented. Production was increased from 450K tonnes per year to 650K tonnes per year. Manpower was reduced from 12 to 6 people per shift by the introduction of new and more efficient engineering integration and technology and computerisation.

Footnote.

When the Arklow manufacturing was ceased in 2002 the Production Manager took up an invitation from Fatima Fertiliser Ltd., in Pakistan to take charge of the recommissioning of CAN 3 at their Plant site in Mukhtar Garh, Sadiqabad in 2009. The recommissioning was satisfactorily completed in 2010 and the Plant is successfully producing 1400 tonnes per day of 27.5% CAN in 2024.

COMPOUND FERTILIZER UNIT

In the compound fertilizer unit, which has a capacity of 100,000 long tons per annum, phosphoric acid, possibly mixed with nitric acid, is neutralized with ammonia.

The use of a concentrator for the mash, especially developed by UHDE, makes previous concentration of the phosphoric acid unnecessary. This arrangement eliminates the problems usually encountered in such plants and simplifies the equipment.

The concentrated granulative mash is mixed with the required amount of potassium salt and granulated. After drying in a rotary dryer, oversize and undersize are separated. The product (2-4 mm. sizes) is finally powdered and transported to the storage.

The plant off -gases are scrubbed in a scrubber, so that the neighbourhood is not molested by ammonia- or fluorine-containing gases. By varying the raw material quantities, a great number of different compound fertilizers can be produced.

CHAPTER 4

BAGGING, LOADING PLANT & STACTING PLANT

Joe Weadick

The two products, ammonium sulphate and ammonium nitrate limestone, are sent to the bagging and loading unit where they are stored in separate stores. A bagging and loading station is available for both products having separate loading facilities for the bagging of AS and ANL and the bulk loading of AS. Both products can be loaded either in rail trucks or road trucks.

The stores for AS and ANL have a capacity of 20,000 long tons each. Discharge from the stores is affected by modern semiautomatic scrapers which are equipped with caterpillars and which can be moved about in the entire store. A well-conceived belt conveying system transfers the products automatically to the bagging statins which are equipped with most modern weighing and bagging facilities and which have a capacity of 500 to 625 cwt – bags per hour, i.e. 25 to 31.25 long tons/hr, each. The products can be filled alternatively in open plastic bags, which are sealed by welding machines, or in halved bags. For the loading of AS the desired carrying capacity is adjusted on the loading ramp after which the wagons or lorries are loaded fully automatically. The loading of bags is accomplished without manual operation. A dedusting system ensures clean, dust-free filling of the bag.

Before fork-trucks and palletizers became available three operators were required to load the bags. One person taking a bag off the conveyor chute coming from the plant, a second person taking the bag off the operator who took it off the conveyor and handed it to a third operator who placed it in position on the truck or railcar. This system became unnecessary when the fork-trucks and palletizers arrived.

I remember a fire started in one of the bagging platforms once. The operators had closed down the bagging machines and went to lunch in their messroom which was in the same plant area as the bagging machines. One of the operators heard something as he was eating his lunch, got up and opened the messroom door. He saw one of the bagging platforms on fire. He sounded the fire alarm immediately and the Fire engine and crew arrived within minutes. They got the electricity switched off. Two crew members put on breathing apparatus and used CO_2 and Dry Powder fire extinguishers to put the fire out which they succeeded in about fifteen minutes. An investigation took place to find out what caused the fire and it was found that someone unknown had put a piece of wood in the housing of one of the bagging machines. Why this was done was never found out.

The Stacking Area workers were:

Mick Murray senior operator.

Jack Byrne operator.

Richie Price operator.

Michael Doyle operator.

John Osborne day operator.

These operators used forklift trucks to load the train, all trucks and brought the pallets to the stacking storage area.

CHAPTER 5

WELFARE

Joe Weadick

There were two large Nissan huts (each about 80 ft long and 30 ft wide) situated opposite the laboratory building on the north side of the open drain. They were used for various reasons when building the factory. When their original use was finished with the one nearest the drain was used as the factory canteen. The second one was used for the electrical workshop (east half) and Instrument workshop (west half).

This was the position until the second three story office building was completed in about 1969. The factory canteen was then transferred to the ground floor of the new Adm Two. The Nissan hut vacated was then used as a maintenance shop for all factory machinery.

If my memory is correct, I believe the road from Kilbride down to the back gate was completed and put to use in 1968. A security/weighbridge office and a weighbridge was built at the back-gate so that goods and fertilizer trucks could use it.

When I became Welfare Officer in 1974 I had two shift security men on each gate and one safety/security man on each shift checking all the breathing apparatus, gas masks, fire extinguishers etc. through-out the factory, as well as routine security checks on each plant. Any problems with any equipment or security incidents had to be reported to my day foreman and have repairs carried out. I discussed with my foreman on a daily basis any repairs required or fire extinguishers refilled or replaced.

In 1975 it was decided by factory management that a new 300-Seater factory canteen was required to cater for the rising number of staff. As Welfare Officer I was involved in the design of the new canteen with our caterers Campbell Catering. We visited a number of canteens in Dublin as well as Canteen Kitchen Equipment suppliers to ensure we get the best equipment for our new canteen.

The new canteen was completed and opened in about 1976. The canteen was transferred from Adm 2. The electrical and instrument departments transferred from the Nissan hut to Adm 2 where the canteen had been.

Around the same time a new welfare building was built for all the maintenance staff. It comprised of a locker room with 145 double lockers, a drying room with 145 single lockers, a shower room with six showers, a wash room with 45 sinks and 10 toilets. All the maintenance staff were delighted with their new facilities. The front door into the facilities was opposite the laboratory building at the north side of the open drain so a foot bridge was built to access the building from the pathway.

A new garage was also built on the west side of Adm 2. The two nissan huts were taken down and removed.

Welfare Attendants - Willie Kavanagh.

Sean Kinsella.

Chisty Rock.

Breda Byrne.

Angela Redmond.

Plus, sixteen other Welfare Attendants.

CHAPTER 6

SECURITY

Joe Weadick

Our security Officer was Dermot O'Sullivan who previously was an officer in the Irish army before working in NET. I believe he was not well and I visited him in his home on Ferrybank Arklow on a few occasions. He and his wife told me he suffered from Angina. Soon after I last visited him he took bad and was brought to hospital where he died.

I recommended Seamus Delaney who was an operator in the 1500 unit, for the job, and he was successful. Seamus was in the Irish army before working in NET. I believe he also spent some time as a Police Officer in (I think) Nigeria in Africa while he was in the army. He reported to me and I was satisfied he would make a good security officer.

He worked hard at the security job and he had one case where a number of outside complaints about a member of the sales and distribution department resulted in that person being terminated in the position. Seamus was not very long in the job when he decided to take his redundancy to look after his own business in Woodenbridge.

I had a very serious case where a store-man in the stores department was terminated for stealing from the company.

In another case I got a call from the Bray Gardai that they searched a large van they found broken down on the road near Bray with three persons in it. They found the van full of aluminium sheets, confiscated it and drove it to the Bray Garda station where they made the men unload the sheets. I went to Bray, identified the sheets and was asked to send a lorry from our factory to collect the load as soon as possible. The sheets had been taken from the oil line to the factory from the harbour in the Arklow Marsh.

The fumes from the factory affected farms nearby so much that we had to compensate two farmers and buy one of the farms. We also had to compensate a Mr Proby and buy his estate in Ballyraine Arklow.

Our factory maintenance manager was chairman of the local Handy-Caped Persons Organization at the time. NET decided to sell Probys estate to the Handy-Caped People Organisation for one Irish pound which was the correct thing to do. The estate house and out-houses have been updated over the years and is now a major facility for handy-caped people in the Arklow.

The farm we bought and compensated the owner for was Gargans in Glenart Arklow. Part of the compensation for Mr Gargan was a new house in Arklow for his family. The farmer we compensated but did not buy his farm was situated on the north side of the factory and was not as badly affected as those on the south side.

My security function for the company was to visit the farm and estate our company bought, on a regular basis to ensure that no trespassing or damage was being done to the property or land. In Gargans case they left the house and I visited it often and discovered that it was being used by drug users and they plastered the inside walls in the house with all sorts of satanic writing. I had to get the Arklow Gardai to investigate it but they decided that there was very little they could do because the house was in an isolated area.

I had a chat with our civil supervisor in the factory Seamus O'Brien, and we decided the best thing to do was to knock down the house. Our factory manager agreed and we employed a contractor to carry out the work and spread the contents over a bank situated near the old house. Soon after getting rid of the house problem the company decided to plant thousands of trees on the land. I would say that the trees planted would be ready now after all those years, to take down and sell for a good profit.

On the Proby estate there was a large wood situated along the roadside which I checked often, particularly on Saturdays, to ensure that nobody was stealing timber. One Saturday I heard the sound of chainsaws in the wood. I had a good idea what was going on so I rang the Arklow Garda station and the sergeant came out to me. We got over the fence into the wood and walked up to the culprits who were cutting down the trees. They were caught red-handed and prosecuted.

I got on to the Shelton prison warden and asked him to get some guys from the prison to bring a tractor and trailer to the Ballyraine wood and fill the trailer up with the wood that the culprits had cut down, bring the load to the prison and cut the wood into small blocks for firewood. It can be given out at Christmas to poor people. The Shelton prison was used to cutting wood for poor people at Christmas.

The company also bought the two cottages at the entrance to Glenart Castle.

We arranged for Arklow Vincent De Paul to house poor people requiring somewhere to live, into the left cottage. The right cottage was in fact the gate lodge into the castle. We decided to leave that vacant for the castle owners.

The family, who were living in the left cottage had to be compensated and given a new home.

Security Observation.

One occasion I went out to the factory at night to observe the area of the back gate for possible burglars entering the factory to steal equipment from the main stores which was located east of the back gate and vulnerable to any burglar trying to enter the site at night.

I decided to go up to the roof of Admin 2 where I would have a wider area to check. I was there beside the roof water tank for about a half hour when I saw two figures approaching me. They were the shift foreman and an operator who had seen something on the roof in the silluette of the lights on the high Acid Tower. When they approached me I realized who they were and explained that I was observing the area of the back gate and the fence east of there because it was a handy area for some burglar to get over the fence with a view to breaking into the stores and stealing equipment. I said it was so dark on the roof that I never thought anyone could see me. They said they saw my figure shining in the lights on top of the acid tower. We chatted for a while and came down.

In the front gate which was manned around the clock we had a buzzer that would activate and you could speak through a microphone if someone came to the back gate at night. On occasion people did drive down to the back gate at night the buzzer was activated and the security man would speak through the microphone which made those people drive away.

After that event I decided to observe from somewhere more secretive.

Security of Jobs

From the time the building of NET was started in 1962, people from all over the county of Wicklow, Wexford and even the east part of Carlow were applying for jobs in the factory. The first Irish Company to get a contract was Irish Engineering Co, who got the contract to have an embankment built right around the site to prevent flooding because of the soft marsh type ground in the area.

The four Irish Enco. Employees to open the gate into the site were Seamus O'Brien from Clara Vale, Sean McLoughlin from Rathdrum, Tony Hobbs from Gorey and Bill Keogh from Avoca. Those four people were subsequently employed by NET even before the factory was ready for production in 1965.

Jobs in the factory were being filled from 1964 onwards as plants were ready for production, until it reached about thirteen hundred in 1975. As well as NET staff there was always about two hundred contractors working on site at this stage.

The wages/salaries paid to employees were very good compared to what people were being paid in most other company's and this situation continued right up to the time the company went bankrupt in 2002, even though the staff continued to be reduced from 1982 when the Ammonia Plant shut down.

The high wages being paid in NET resulted in Arklow being one of the most expensive towns in Ireland to shop. Even now in 2024 the town is still very expensive to shop in. Even the closure of the Avoca Mines in 1981, the closure of Arklow Pottery/Noritaki in the late nineties. The closure of Quality Ceramics and other smaller companies, and of course the devastating bankruptcy of IFI in 2002.

Transport of Gauzes from the Airport to our factory

I remember one day seeing a package of our platinum gauze arriving at the back gate security with an expensive car behind it with four security men in it. I spoke to the manager about it and he said it was the normal procedure because of the cost of the gauze which could be from a half to one million pounds. I felt having all these security men with the gauze was only advertising the fact to any burglars who planned to steal it.

I had a meeting with the factory manager about it and we decided, in future to hire a local courier to go to the airport with one of our security men accompanying him wearing his personal clothes, no uniform. The only stipulation we told the courier was to go straight to the airport and back without stopping for any other goods. This was agreed and we never had any trouble since.

The Acid Plant Manager told me that on one occasion before we changed the procedure, they employed an armed Arklow Garda to stay in the Nitric Acid Control Room over night when gauze was there.

CHAPTER 7

SAFETY

Joe Weadick

In 1977 our present safety advisor became ill with a heart problem and had to retire from the factory. I was recommended for the safety advisor position by the outgoing safety advisor Tom Seale and was successful in getting the job.

I liked Tom very much and was sorry that he had to leave. He had been the safety advisor in the mines in western Australia for a number of years and came back to Ireland to take up the safety advisor's job in the Avoca Mines in the late fifties. The mines closed in the early sixties so Tom applied for and got the safety advisors job in NET. He used to train young people Tac-Wan-Do in the KB hall in Ferrybank when he was in the fertilizer factory.

He lived in Templerainey almost opposite the school. He and his wife told me the story about one of his sons who fell off a roof in India when he was touring that country and died. A terrible tragedy. Tom had a friend in India who arranged to have Tom's sons body brought home.

I started in the Fire & Safety Advisors job in 1977. My responsibilities were:

To assist and advise management in the implementation and maintenance of the company S.H. & E Policy.

To monitor the implementation of the Policy and report on departures from agreed methods and standards.

To co-ordinate the drawing up of Factory Safety Procedures and Permanent Instructions and to assist management as required.

To draw up an Emergency Plan and test the Plan.

To monitor all safety aspects of shutdown work and ensure that IFI and contractor employees are adequately briefed on safety matters and working safely.

To ensure site safety equipment is serviceable and adequately maintained.

To liaise with local authorities and Statutory Bodies on fire and safety matters.

To provide appropriate safety training courses for site personnel and contractors.

To participate in investigation of serious accidents/incidents and monitor remedial actions.

The first job I did in my new position as Fire & Safety Advisor was to get permission from the factory manager to make the wearing of eye protection a standard safety rule for all staff working on plants and in maintenance departments. It cost the company a lot of money but very necessary. I actually gave a prize to any worker I met while walking around the site if they had their safety glasses until everyone got used to the idea of wearing them.

The second job I did was to make the wearing of helmets a standard safety rule for all staff on plants and in maintenance departments.

I declared that the same rules applied to office staff when they visited plants, maintenance departments or the stores.

At the time the compulsory wearing of eye protection and helmets were not covered by any legislation and I got a lot of criticism from contractors working on site. It even went as far as protesting letters to our company from contractor companies maintaining that the wearing of helmets was unsafe in their profession. I told contractor personnel during my safety talk with them that they must abide by our safety rules or they could not come on site. It was not long before the wearing of helmets became the law.

I carried out my duties by having a standard monthly program of drawing up the total monthly accidents, broken down to each plant and each department, showing minor accidents and lost time accidents. We used the international system of lost time accidents of one day absent from work or more. I always included the names of the workers who had the accidents

Together with the analysis of the monthly accidents I wrote a one-page account of the accidents/injuries that occurred, commenting on the possible reason why they occurred and advised on the best action to avoid such accidents/injuries occurring again. All the time encouraging our staff to work safely at all times.

I was the secretary of the factory safety committee which also sat monthly and discussed the accidents/injuries/incidents. It also discussed what work was required to be done as a result of the items listed on my plant inspections which I carried out periodically. Generally, our safety record was good but unfortunately, we had one fatal accident just a few months after I became safety advisor.

It happened in the CCF plant on a day when the plant was shut down to clean off the build-up of cacked fertilizer from the inside of the approximately 80 ft. long horizontal conveyor with steel chains circulating through it. The plant was shut-down in the morning, electrically isolated and a number of the side panels were removed by the fitters to allow access for the plant operators to get inside to remove the cacked fertilizer. It was agreed between the maintenance foreman and the process foreman to reconnect the machine and let it run to get rid of the loose fertilizer during lunch-time.

Unfortunately, when all the plant and maintenance workers had left the plant, the plant engineer and his supervisor, unknown to the senior operator who was in the control room arranging for the electrician to reconnect the conveyor, decided while walking down the site from the engineer's office in Adm. 1 to go into the plant from a back door, up the stairs and the engineer decided to get into the conveyor without going to the control room which was about 80 ft away, to look for a permit which they could not have got. The conveyor ran along a platform about 8 ft above the floor. The engineer's supervisor was on the platform looking in at the engineer when the operator walked up to the switch and started the conveyor.

Seconds later he turned the conveyor off when the supervisor shouted down that the engineer was inside the conveyor. It was too late for the engineer who was crushed to death in that short time. It was a terrible tragedy for the engineer's family, a terrible tragedy for the company and a terrible tragedy for me just starting my new job.

We, NET, was brought to Arklow District Court by the Factory Inspector and given a fine of 50 Irish pounds on a technicality of not having padlocks in our 'Work Permit Procedure', even though our company was regarded as being one of the safest companies in Ireland, particularly our Work Permit Procedures. At the time personal padlocks for every worker was not widely known.

The investigation was carried out by myself and my manager and we came to the conclusion that,

1. There should have been a standby operator on duty at the conveyor during the lunch break to ensure nobody would get into it.

2. When the operator was going to switch on the conveyor, he should have walked the full length of the machine to ensure no-one had arrived at it from the back stairs.

3. It will be emphasized at every opportunity that all staff, including engineers and managers must comply with the Work Permit System.

4. All staff to be given their own padlock which must be attached to the equipment they are working on and the equipment must not be electrically connected until everyone's padlock has been removed.

5. The Safety Advisor, myself, to arrange purchase of the padlocks and have them distributed. He will also do regular checks in work situations to ensure the system is being operated correctly.

The Engineer's name was Jim O'Callaghan who I knew well. He was a Dublin man but married to a Gorey girl and lived in Ballymoney Courtown. He was a brilliant saxophone player and at the time of the accident and his death he was the saxophone player with the Coolgreaney Jazz Band. The other members were Andy Cusack piano player, one of our senior managers in NET, Jim Tyrrell trumpet player and leader, his brother Michael was the bass guitar player, Pat McCarthy Trombone player and George Byrne drummer. Jim & Michael Tyrrell and George Byrne were also members with me in the Columbia Showband.

Jim's brother Freddy was an officer in the Army School of Music in Rathmines Dublin and actually gave me several lessons on the trombone I was learning when I was in the Army School of Music In 1956. Another brother of Jim was Peter who at the time was working in our Drawing office.

It was very sad but I must mention that when I was planning to leave the Columbia Showband in 1965 to look for a job in NET. I asked Pat who was a friend of mine, would he take my place in the band because I did not want to leave the boys without a trombone player. Believe it or not Pat was already working in an office in NET for two months. His father, who was a wheelchair person working for the Transport Workers Union in Arklow had got Pat, his son, the job in NET. Pat really wanted to take the position but when he asked his father's permission his father nearly hit the roof because of all the work he had done to get him the job. Pat told his father that music was his life and after some hours his father relented with a lot of persuasion from Pats mother and gave him permission. Pat has been a professional Trombone player ever since, over 60 years.

Over the years there were only two serious accidents. The first one took place in Nitric Acid No.4. plant. It happened very simply when the senior operator climbed up about eight feet on a ladder to retrieve a light- steel tube off the roof of the control room for an operator when the ladder slipped down onto the floor and the senior operator fell sideways hitting off a large table placed nearby. He broke his back and has been crippled for years. He walks now with the aid of a stick. Very unfortunate for him and his family. I am delighted to say that I recommended that our insurance company look after him, which they did.

The other very serious accident happened to an operator in the 1500 Unit palletizer shed. He noticed that one bag had gone sideways on the table. He thought it would be ok to get in over the safety rail and straighten the bag but got caught by the bag which got stuck. He was unable to move and was scared that the steel table the bags were on would move and seriously injure him. The electrician was called and he managed to isolate the palletizer without the table moving. The operator got out but was shocked and suffered mental problems for a long time. He made a mistake in getting over the safety rail but I recommended that he too be looked after by our insurance company and they did, which I was delighted about.

We had one very distressing case when the senior operator in the CAN Plant, went missing on his last night shift before Christmas. The operators working that night searched everywhere on the plant and eventually I was called out and arrived at 6.AM. As I arrived at the CAN plant the operators there told me they just found him hanging from a small thin rope about 80 ft up on the top of the plant - dead. He had committed suicide. This was terrible news for everyone on the plant and everyone in the factory. Like everyone else I was shocked. It was such a terrible thing to happen just before Christmas and he was such a good senior operator and well-liked by everybody in the factory. He was married with a wife and two children, from and living in Gorey.

Our fire crew were so distressed I had to call out the Arklow Fire Brigade to get his body down which was not an easy thing because he was hanging from a pipe between the two plants and was very difficult to get at. However, the firemen managed it after some time.

I had to call the Gardai out which they did and I identified the body for them. I also called the undertaker to take the body to the hospital for a post mortem. It was the saddest event I was part of for the entire time I was safety advisor.

About six months later our Personnel Manager and I attended Coronors Court

Inquest in Wicklow and Peters wife appreciated and thanked us for attending.

Peter once climbed Mount Killimanjaro in Tanzania with a group from Gorey for charity. A seat with his name on it was placed outside the Lodge in Glenmalure in his memory.

I formed a factory Safety Quiz Team of three members and they turned out to be excellent. I acted as their manager and we took part in many competitions outside our factory. One year we came a close second in a major quiz in Dublin which was a great achievement, not just for the team members and myself as manager, but also for our factory.

FACTORY INSPECTORATE

The Factory Inspector carried out inspections of the factory approximately every year without prior notification. When he arrived at our factory, I would welcome him and accompany him around the site to inspect where he wished. I would not try to tell him where to inspect, that was his prerogative. If he found anything of concern, he would discuss with me how it should be rectified. We would always receive a report of his visit with recommendations, if necessary.

Apart from the monthly safety committee meeting I carried out safety meetings with all sections of workers on a three-monthly basis, where I would discuss any accidents that occurred in their plant/area and how to ensure the accidents would not happen again. These meetings were always very positive.

All our fire team members had to be first aiders also, so I organized first aid competitions in co-operation with the First Aid teacher I hired. The competitions took place in the Arklow Bay Hotel and teams from other factories also took part. They were great in keeping our first aiders up to date.

I attended the annual safety conference every year and was allowed by the factory manager to bring two safety committee members. We travelled to the conference the evening before it started and travelled home the evening after it finished. It was always a valuable experience for my safety committee colleagues and myself.

FIRE PROTECTION

We had our own Fire Tender and Ambulance. I had a fire crew of eight operators on every shift, two of whom would also act as ambulance drivers if the situation arose. I ran four-hour training sessions every Wednesday for the crew members on their rest days. I recorded the attendance of the firemen in a special book. Their accumulated hours were paid at Christmas.

There was one member of my Fire Teams who I must write about and that was Paddy Finn. He has been an Asthmatic sufferer all his life and decided to start the Arklow Asthmatic Society in 1980 to help asthmatics. He felt that learning/playing a musical instrument would be good for their breathing so he started the "Arklow Youth Marching Band in 1988. Before I continue with the Fire Protection Section I now write his compelling and brilliant true story.

1988. Played their 1st outing in the John Holland/Garden of Ireland 4th of July Festival. They also played that year for the President of Ireland at the opening of the new Arklow Lifeboat station. Finally in that year played in their 1st competition in Nobber Co. Meath.

1989. Hosted the Grassy Plains Drum Corps from Bethel, Connecticut, USA.

1990. Travelled to America, played in the famous Yankee Stadium in New York to 50,000 people, which made them their own. They were the only Irish band to play in the Yankee Stadium.

1991. Won the all-Ireland Championship in the Novice Class.

1992. Hosted a band from Bristol in England.

1993. Hosted a band from Delft from Holland. They were also All-Ireland League Champions also in that year.

1994. Toured and played in Denmark, Holland and Poland. They also won the all-Ireland in the Contest Class.

1995/6. Were the winners in the Champion Class.

1988/2012. Played in four St. Patrick's Day Parades in Dublin.

1988/2012. Played in seven Rose of Tralee Festivals.

1988/2012. Led the London/Irish Parade once.

1988/2012. Played in the Birmingham Parade ten times.

1988/2012. Played in Anfield Stadium in Liverpool also the Square.

1988/2012. Played every year in the Arklow St. Patrick's Day Parade.

1988/2012. Played in every county in Ireland.

There was always between fifty and sixty members in the band which included the musicians and the Baton Twirling members.

STATE OF CONNECTICUT EXECUTIVE CHAMBERS, HARTFORD, CONNECTICUT

August 15th 1990

Dear Paddy,

I join with your many friends and neighbors in paying tribute to you and in thanking you for your many contributions to building friendship between people of different nations.

People to people exchanges have proven to be a most effective vehicle for building bridges of cooperation, appreciation and understanding among people of differing backgrounds and cultures.

Over the years, you have been the driving force for mutually beneficial, educational and enjoyable exchanges between the Grassy Plains Drum Corps of Bethel and the Arklow Youth

Marching Band of Arklow, Ireland. In so doing, you have given many young people the opportunity to participate in a program which allows them to explore personal values, work purposefully, and broaden their horizons , and enjoy themselves at the same time.

Your efforts are most appreciated by all who have been privileged to be a part of this excellent exchange program, and by all who see the value in creating an environment where friendship, understanding and peace can flourish.

May you enjoy this well-deserved testimonial in your honor and continue to add to your long record of dedicated service to others for many more years.

With kind regards,

Sincerely,

William A O'Neill

Governor

Best wishes from

IFI

IRISH FERTILIZER INDUSTRIES

Irish Fertilizer Industries Ltd.,

Are the only manufacturer of fertilizer in Ireland, employing over 700 people

And producing

The country's leading brands.

PASTURE SWARD   CUT SWARD

SULPHA SWARD   NET NITRATE

SUPER NET

LEIFI START   LEIFI BOOST

NET UREA   TOPPER

The advertisement was put in the "Arklow Marching Band's book in 1997.

FIRE PROTECTION TRAINING

The training sessions included,

1. Using a fire Hose the correct way.

2. Tackling different types of fires.

3. Wearing breathing apparatus while using fire hose in different types of contaminated areas, for example oil, fertilizer, wood, plastic.

4. Ensuring that electricity is isolated before tackling a fire.

5. Tackling a fire on a height using the fire tender ladders.

6. Wearing full protection suits and wearing breathing apparatus when dealing with an ammonia leak.

The only fire that I can remember where my fire crew was called out to a plant fire happened in Nitric Acid 4 plant. The turbine started smouldering and was red hot. The fire crew had to wear breathing apparatus and put it out with CO_2 and powder fire extinguishers. They could not use water on it.

I do recall a serious fire happening one evening in our tip-head on the north side of Shelton Avenue. It was in the month of March and grass was extremely dry. My factory fire crew was called out to extinguish it but it spread very quickly in the dry grass, and the trees on the north side started burning. It was impossible to put the fire out. We worked all night fighting it and into the next day using water from the canal. We called out the Arklow Fire Brigade the next morning and they continued for a number of hours until they succeeded in getting it out. They put their portable fire pump at the canal and drew water from it, through the pump and supplied the firemen with water. I had stayed with the crew all night and also gave each one of them a rest while I operated the hose. We were very much afraid that the fire would continue burning all the way down the Marsh to Arklow.

We had one great experience when the County Wexford Fire Fighting Teams went on strike. I got a phone call from the late Garda Superintendent in Arklow Peter Finn asking if I could ask for our fire-fighting team to put out a fire in the Coolgreaney village which is six miles from Arklow but in Co. Wexford. As it happened Peter lived in Coolgreaney close to where the fire was. One of our personnel officers, Jack Martin, also lived in the same estate as Peter and also near the fire. I got permission from our factory manager and went to help out. It was a hot summers day and took our fire team fours to put it out. They appreciated our help very much and it was like another fire practice for us.

The gate security man saw an old house on fire up on the bank near Shelton Abbey Forestry Training Centre one night and called out our Fire Team to put it out. There was nobody living in it at the time and it was thought there must have been squatters or someone using drugs in it at some time.

I also remember a fire starting one summer in the trees on the hill outside the back gate before I left the ammonia plant. It burned for about one week and was dealt with by the Arklow fire brigade. The late

Dermot O'Sullivan was the security officer at the time and kept an eye on the fire on the bank to make sure it would not affect the factory.

One last incident I went to see happened on the main road near 'Jack Whites' pub. A business man, on his way to a meeting in Dublin got a heart attack and crashed into the side of a fertilizer truck on its way from our Belfast factory to our Arklow factory. The car went on fire and stopped on his own side of the road. The driver of the car, who was on his own, burned to death.

Due to the impact with the car, a number of the pallets of fertilizer fell onto the road and the gardai were on the scene also, directing traffic. The late Dave Brady, who was the manager in the Bagging & Loading plant at the time, and a colleague of mine, arrived on the scene after me to see what happened and I filled him in. Needless to say he was shocked at the sight of the dead man whose body was burnt to a cinder. The Arklow undertaker was called by the gardai to come out and take the body to Loughlinstown hospital for a post-mortem. The truck driver was alright except that he was also shocked at the scene. Dave contacted a local farmer to come and take all the spilled fertilizer off the road and put it into one of his fields, and keep it for himself without charge. Peter Finn was at the scene also directing his gardai staff but had no mobile phone with him. In those days a mobile phone was big with a pack of batteries and contained in a leather bag with a shoulder strap on it. I gave him a loan of mine which he appreciated.

Over the years I organized Fire Crew competitions, most of the time the competition would be held in our factory. They were very well attended and were proven to be worthwhile from a training viewpoint. My team won a few times. The Shearing Plough factory in Rathdrum were an excellent team and won a number of times. We had between six and eight teams taking part every year. The fire Team from our Marino Point Plant took part once. We also had a team from MSD take part one year. They were very enjoyable events.

HARBOUR INCIDENT

One day in the 1980's the factory emergency alarm activated. I rang Security and asked what was the problem. The Security man told me that an incident has happened at Arklow Harbour. I called out the Fire Crew and we took the Fire brigade out and travelled to the harbour. Going up the back road from the factory the fire engine stalled and we had to get it going again. We got going but it took some time to get to the harbour and arrived there via Seaview Avenue. As we passed Arklow Engineering Services we noted a number of their workers at their main entrance looking across at our harbour compound. We stopped at the compound and inquired from one of our harbour operators what has happened and was told that a ship load of UAN (urea/Ammonia/Nitrate mixture) of liquid fertilizer had arrived and the ship's crew started pumping the UAN into our tank when a vacuum was created in the tank and resulted in an implosion that collapsed the tank roof. When the ship's crew realized what was happening, they immediately stopped pumping the UAN.

It was unknown why it happened so it was decided to return the ship with its cargo. Our company decided not to continue with the project and that was the end of it.

36

ALL the Arklow councilors criticized us, NET, over the incident for months and compared NET with the Nuclear Plant in Wales.

One good thing happened on the day of the incident a, that was the problem we had with the Fire Brigade engine stalling as we travelled to the harbour. I got permission from the factory manager to buy an up-to-date fire engine to replace the existing one. Within two months I bought a good second-hand automatic Fire Engine which lasted us very well up to the shutdown in 2002.

OPERATOR FOUND DEAD AT THE HARBOUR.

There was one very sad incident at the harbour. One of the harbour operators was found dead in the compound one morning. When the operators were getting ready to go off shift one person was not in the locker room. Two operators went looking for him and found him lying on the ground beside the ammonia pump dead. I was called down to investigate the situation and like the operators I agreed with them that he must have suffered a heart attack, fell on the ground and passed away. I had to call the Gardai and explain the situation and they agreed what happened. A post mortem was carried out in the hospital and confirmed that it was a heart attack.

NITRIC ACID FUMES INCIDENT

I got a complaint one day from one of our workers that his car which he parked in the carpark near the canteen and there was a number of marks on his car and thought it came from nitric acid fumes on the startup of the plant. I investigated the complaint and decided that were twelve marks on the car and decided they were caused by the nitrous fumes on start-up. I then checked all the cars there and agreed that a total of eleven cars were badly marked and arranged for all eleven affected cars to be repainted.

BAD SMELL COMPLAINT

I got a phone call one night from Security to inform me that a resident in Mountain Bay Estate, rang to report that there was a bad smell in his area and he reckoned it was from NET. I rang Terry Spacey and we both drove to his house, spoke to him and his wife and explained that a northerly wind was and is blowing which meant that it was imposable to be coming from the factory. We suggested that it may be a farmer spreading big slurry on his land. After further discussion they agreed with us and said good night.

It was an important part of Terry Spacey and my job to follow-up any complaints about smells coming from the factory which we took seriously. We often checked in the town at night to see if there were any smells and on occasion we got slight ammonia smells, which we followed up in the factory and found that on occasion the vent was slightly open on one of the spheres to reduce the pressure slightly. We told the ammonia plant staff to make sure that the vents were kept closed at all times.

1987 – HURRICANE CHARLIE

A very bad stormy night occurred in the winter of 1987 (called after Charlie Haughty). The factory internal road was badly flooded with the heavy rain.

It was so bad that we were worried that the ammonia pump motor under the sphere would get flooded causing problems up the site. I drove out to the factory and called out the fire team to go to the sphere, prepare two fire hoses and pump the rain water over the embankment from the ground under the sphere to prevent the water flooding the ammonia pump. I walked up the steps at the water treatment plant to the top of the embankment and saw the river the water back over the embankment for four hours until the river water level subsided.

The train from Dublin to Arklow was only travelling at a snail's pace. The train stopped at the factory and myself and gonead few others got on and got a lift home to Arklow. I left my car at the factory until the following day.

TRANSPORT OF LARGE NITRIC ACID TOWER AND ASSOCIATED TANKS FROM ARKLOW HARBOUR

This was a major operation which was never seen in Arklow before. We had a number of meetings on site to plan the event. It was attended by representatives of: the company contracted to transport the tower and associated tanks, ESB, Posts & telegraphs, Wicklow County Council, the Arklow Gardai, the Factory Manager and myself.

The tower was about one hundred feet long and about twenty feet in diameter.

It meant that all ESB cables and all telephone cables had to be removed over the road to allow the tower and convoy of tanks to pass and replaced after the convoy had gone. It was a lot of work for the staff of the ESB and P & T.

I had to arrange six generators for shops along the way. I also arranged a canteen in the Sports Centre on Seaview Avenue for all people living along Ferrybank and Templerainey who wanted to have breakfast.

All man hole covers along the way had to be covered with eight by four feet steel sheets to protect the covers.

The tower was secured on a special undercarriage with about forty double wheels on either side. There were a number of the contract staff walking on both sides of the tower and the rest of the convoy to ensure all was OK and to keep the people walking along with it kept at a safe distance. It moved at about one mile per hour which meant that it took about three hours to reach the factory. It left the harbour at about 0500 hrs on a beautiful June Sunday morning in I think, 1992. The townspeople enjoyed the special event very much. It was, indeed, a first for Arklow and we might never witness another such event.

AMMONIA INFORMATION SHEET – ISSUED TO RESIDENTS LIVING WITHIN 1.5 KILOMETERS OF THE FACTORY CONFORMING WITH DIRECTIVE No. 82/501/EEC

ANHYDROUS AMMONIA

Formula NH3

Ammonia is the basis for all nitrogen fertilizers and is manufactured for this purpose by Irish Fertilizer industries at Marino Point, Cork with natural gas as the basic raw material.

For over sixty years, ammonia has been in common use throughout the world as a major industrial chemical. Currant world production is about ninety million tonnes per year and in some countries like America and Britain, ammonia is injected directly into the soil.

In Ireland, ammonia has been used in fertilizer production for many years. Irish Fertilizer Industries has been producing and processing ammonia in Ireland since 1965, and is fully experienced in the safety aspects of producing and handling the product.

Ammonia is present in small concentrations in water, earth and particularly in decomposing organic matter. It is the product of normal, animal and plant metabolism and of primary importance in the nitrogen metabolism of plants.

It is also familiar in the home in a dilute form as smelling salts and is contained in some household window and floor cleaning fluids.

Storage and transportation

Ammonia is normally stored and transported either,

At atmospheric pressure and under refrigeration – such as in the Marino Point storage facilities or,

Under pressure at ambient temperature – as at Irish Fertilizers, Arklow and in rail car transportation.

Ammonia is a colourless liquid which boils at - 33°C to give a colourless gas.

The liquid is totally mixable with water and the gas is very soluble in water. The liquid is about two-thirds the density of water and the vapour is about two-thirds the density of air.

Ammonia is always produced, stored and transported in completely enclosed systems so that any hazard can only arise in the event of a leak or spill. Like other chemicals, it can be hazardous, but the long history of production and usage has led to the development of comprehensive procedures for its safe production and handling. Ammonia is generally a non-flammable chemical.

Ammonia gas can have a pungent penetrating odour depending on the concentration of the gas in air. The gas can be a strongly irritant chemical and in high enough concentration it can produce irritation of the eyes and mucous membrane in the respiratory tract.

Because of these disagreeable characteristics, it is unlikely that anyone would voluntarily remain in an atmosphere contaminated with ammonia gas.

What concentrations are we talking about ?

There is a technical term called the Threshold Limit Value, or TLV for short, which defines the concentration of ammonia gas in air under which it is believed that nearly all workers may be repeatedly exposed day after day without adverse effect. This TLV is set out by a totally independent body called the American Conference of Government Industrial Hygienists and is used by the Irish Department of Labour.

The value is expressed as parts of ammonia gas in one million parts of air i.e. p.p.m for short.

The TLV for ammonia is 25 p.p.m. The following table indicates the effect of various concentrations of ammonia gas in the air.

10-15 p.p.m. – the smell of ammonia can be detected by most people.

25 p.p.m. - prolonged repeated exposure causes no injury to the average worker.

Concentrations of (200-300 p.p.m.) will cause irritation and discomfort.

High concentrations (above 2000 p.p.m.) can damage and destroy tissue, particularly tract and moist areas of the body.

Ammonia does not have a cumulative effect on the body.

What to do if exposed to Ammonia

Upon exposure to ammonia, it is important to move from the contaminated area promptly, which would tend to be a person's natural reaction. In the case of contact of the liquid with the eyes or skin, immediate flushing with large quantities of running water is imperative and this should continue for at least 15 minutes. If in any doubt as to whether you've had contact with the liquid, particularly in eyes, go through the washing process to be on the safe side. In all cases of severe injury, a doctor should be called immediately. If the exposure has been slight, usually no treatment will be required but a doctor should be called. In the case of severe exposure to higher concentrations, oxygen may be administered by a person trained to do so. If the patient is not breathing, artificial respiration should be started immediately.

In a situation where a person being exposed to ammonia cannot move from the contaminated area, he or she should go into or remain in a building of solid structure, close the doors and windows, block up the fireplace and switch off any air conditioning units. If the doors and windows are loose-fitting, it would help to block up the openings with wet clothes to help prevent the ingress of ammonia. If, despite the above precautions, some ammonia does get into the room, a person can breathe through a wet cloth to help further. The person should remain in the building until he or she is satisfied that the ammonia atmosphere has cleared or until help arrives.

When the ammonia atmosphere outside is clear again the person should ventilate the building to remove any smell of ammonia which may have got inside.

For the most part, if leaks of ammonia occurred, they would have a localized effect within a production or storage area, and be dealt with by trained personnel. Ammonia can cause severe burns, but this is a hazard of concern mainly to personnel directly involved in operations using the chemical.

Irish Fertilizer Industries

Staff engaged in ammonia production and handling are all trained in the appropriate safety procedures.

This leaflet provides basic information about the chemical, ammonia, and is issued in the interest of public information. It is not intended as a comprehensive safety document.

Further information may be obtained from the company's Safety Advisor.

Issued to residents in the area of the Arklow factory

Conforming with EEC Directive No. 82/501/EEC

Because our factory stores up to 3000 tons of ammonia, the safety advisor must notify every premises within 1.5 km radius with the information contained above every three years. For this purpose, an A4 sheet has been drawn up and a copy of the Ammonia Information Sheet is contained on it.

I visited every house, farm and factory within the 1.5 kilometers once every three years and handed them the A 4 sheet with all the information about ammonia on it and asked if they were happy with the information and knew what to do if any leak of ammonia ever occurred on the plant. They always said they were satisfied with the information and know what steps they would take.

TRANSPORT OF AMMONIA BY RAIL FROM MARINO POINT TO OUR ARKLOW PLANT.

When the Marino Point plant was built a schedule of three trains per day five days per week, each with six ammonia rail cars containing 50 tons of liquid ammonia in each rail car, were transported to the Arklow plant and the three trains returned with the rail cars empty but with approximately 5 atm pressure of ammonia vapour in each. Depending on requirements of ammonia in Arklow, extra trains would be sent on the weekends.

Because of the hazards of ammonia liquid it was necessary to educate all firemen and their superiors and all gardai in the counties that the ammonia trains pass through, of those hazards and the action to take in the event of a serious leak of ammonia from one of the trains.

Myself, as Safety Advisor of the Arklow Plant, a representative of the safety department in Irish Rail and Michael Halford of Irish Rail who carried safety and fire equipment required for our demonstrations. The literature we brought was A4 leaflets similar to what I brought to the residents that live within 1.5 kilometers of the Arklow plant.

In the early nineties myself and the safety representative from Irish rail had a

"An Ammonia Transport Film" professionally produced and gave a copy to each representative of the fire teams and gardai we visited each year. It was an excellent film and showed the ammonia railcars getting loaded with ammonia in Marino Point and getting offloaded in Arklow. It also showed liquid ammonia in a drum in Arklow proving that it was very difficult to ignite and then would not stay on fire.

The only accident we had with the ammonia train was in Hueston Station in Dublin on the way to Arklow. The train had to be changed onto a different track there and go through an underground line to get to the east rail line in Connolly station, to continue on to Arklow. The lever on the track in Hueston station was changed too soon and the last railcar went on the wrong rail-line. It resulted in the back two wheels of the ammonia railcar breaking off as well as the inlet/outlet lines on the railcar. It meant that the only thing stopping the railcar from leaking the ammonia was the non-return valve inside the bottom of the vessel. If it had failed the result for everyone living in the vicinity of Hueston station would have been very badly affected. Thank God it did not fail. I visited the scene the morning after it happened and it was a great shock to me to see what happened. I reported back to our factory manager who was similarly taken aback. Arrangements were made to have the railcar repaired and brought back to Marino Point.

CHAPTER 8

ENGINEERING & CIVIL MAINTENANCE

Tom Mulhall & Joe Weadick

Factory Manager

Bill Flood

Managers

Jim White

Seamus Coughlan

Peter Whelan

Engineers

Pat Crotty

Tony McCaughey

Brian Doyle

Brian Cleary

Gary Richardson

Greg O'Malley

Jim Short

Liam O'Cleirigh

Paddy Madigan

Trevor Hoyle

Declan Wixted

Supervisors

Mick Burke

John Carroll

Tom Copeland

Jim Redmond

Ben Kohler

Terry Hayes

Dave Boddy

Hugh Trainor

Pat O'Leary

Foreman

Pascal Foley

John Cullen

Owen Lynch

Liam Doyle

Mick Kenney

Frank Carroll

John Ryan

Tom Breen

Sean Cannon

Tom Carroll

John Waters

Tom Watters

Paddy O'Brien

George Steele

Dermot Hann

Maintenance Fitter

Larry Noctor

Alan Owens

John Brennan

Paul Brennan

Billy Cowman

Jim Kinsella

Mick Simpson

Danny Byrne

John O'Riordan

Owen Byrne

Aidan Somers

Tom Cullen

Matt Canavan

Pat Duffin

Noel O'Flaherty

Lar Cullen

Tom Connors

Benny Ireton

Mick McGlynn

Jim Malone

New Kealy

John Connolly

Kevin Doyle

Paddy Scanlon

Paddy Swords

John Byrne

Gerry Kavanagh

Har Donnelly

Bill Henry

Jimmy Doyle

Jimmy Clarke

Jimmy Doyle

Bert Sycamore

Ned Behan

Ned Farrell

Jimmy Wolahan

John Gettings

Jim Crofton

Tommy Rowland

ENGINEERING MAINTENANCE PROCEDURES

There are approximately four fitters assigned to each of the Nitric Acid plants on a daily basis, four fitters assigned to the Phosphoric Acid plant on a daily basis and six fitters assigned to the Roaster Plant on a daily basis. Six fitters assigned to the CAN plants on a daily basis, two fitters assigned to the Bagging & Loading plant on a daily basis and about six fitters assigned to the Ammonia Plant on a daily basis. If any work was required to be done at the harbour one of the Bagging & Loading fitters would be sent down to do the work. In the Maintenance workshop where would be a fitter repairing valves, a fitter working at equipment on the machine. Two welders working in the welding section, at a at a minimum. The maintenance workshop foremen and supervisor would be kept very busy organising the work and ensuring sufficient equipment is available.

This arrangement is only for normal daily work where all plants are on line.

All these plants would have a fitter foreman organising the work for his fitters in consultation with each process plant foreman. Normally a list of the work required on the following day will be brought to the area supervisor by the maintenance foreman who will organise the work equipment required for the specific jobs and to make sure that the maintenance foremen have delegated a sufficient number of fitters and helpers. It is vitally important that the fitters and helpers get a work permit for each job before they are allowed to work on it.

Where any plant has a shutdown on a given day or days for inspections of equipment, changing gauzes in reactors, inspecting towers etc. a lot more fitters and helpers would be required. Depending of the number of extra fitters and helpers required it would mean the other plants would have to do with less fitters for the period of the shutdown.

In a plant shutdown situation, some engineers would be involved to carry out inspection, modifications etc. and other very valuable work.

The Ammonia Plant annual shutdown would last up to two weeks and would require contractors to be hired in. Up to forty NET fitters and helpers would be required to get through the quantity of work required. The maintenance supervisors and engineers would be planning the jobs and time required for up to three months beforehand.

Apart from pumps and compressors needing detailed inspections a number of towers would need internal inspections to ensure that there was no internal corrosion which would be serious and may require sections of the towers repaired or renewed.

The Air Separation takes three days to be ready to open up the tanks and vessels for inspection and repairs where necessary. The perlite would have to be replaced which is a major job in itself. When all jobs were complete it would take three days to get the plant up running and ready to send O_2 to the gasification and send N_2 to the 800 unit to produce ammonia.

So, this explanation on how the engineering department works Is just a quick resume of its value to the company. As mentioned above Work Permits, Entry Permits or Excavation Permits may be required. No work can begin without them.

FITTERS STRIKE

A fitters strike began on the 5th of October in 1978 and was not resolved until the 1st of February 1979, when it is said that management gave in and raised the fitters to staff status, the same as the Instruments had. My view was that the fitters claim was right. Their skills would be the same as the Instrument Technicians. I only hope the Electricians were also put on staff status.

Civil Department

Manager

Tony Hobbs .

Foreman

Peter Mooney

Mick Lennon

Felix Byrne

Eddie Gethings

Carpenter

Tony Hobbs

Jim Morris

Painters

Paddy Stokes

Tom Kinch

Kevin Barr

Scaffolders

Tom Collins

Frank Hunt

Mick Osbourne

Mick Dempsey

Willie Morris

Seamus Byrne

Sid Brennan

Tom Keogh

Joe Dowling

Hughie Keogh

John Corr

Raymond Driver

Joe Douglas

Utility Department

Sam Keogh

Seamus Mulhall

Tom Sheridan

Patsy Doyle

Jimmy Conroy

Dick Doyle

Bill Kavanagh

Eamonn Burke

John Byrne

Danny McDonald

Eamonn McDonald

John McDonald

Paddy Byrne

Tom Byrne

Paddy Lacey

Tom McGee

The Civil department is also vital to the engineering maintenance department in supplying them with workers for every situation.

Scaffolders are necessary where any job is done on a height over one meter.

All the scaffolders are kept busy by all the maintenance foreman to make access for the fitters and helpers when working on heights.

The carpenters are also in demand by both maintenance department and the process plants. Mainly required to do work in the stores or in welfare facilities.

The painters are also very necessary workers on site. They may be asked to paint vessels with special paint and may require special protection while painting those particular vessels.

The one very important person to make sure that work carried out is done to the highest standards and safely. These people are the maintenance engineering manager or the Civil manager.

CHAPTER 9

ELECTRICAL & INSTRUMENT DEPT

Joe Weadick

The ESB built a sub-station outside the back gate with 110, kilowatt power supply from Dublin and a 110, kilowatt supply from Waterford. This was done so that if there was a problem from one supply line NET could switch to the other line. Because it was of paramount importance that the factory could depend on a secure power supply at all times.

Seimens Schuckert of Erlangen, got the contract to set up the electrical system throughout the factory. In the planning of the electrical equipment, the principal considerations were given to constant readiness for operation and the maximum safety of all personnel. In all areas where explosive gas-air mixtures could occur, all electrical equipment, including lighting, and communication system, is of explosion-proof design.

All motors and switchgear are enclosed and most of the switchgear is enclosed in special switch-rooms and not exposed to the influence of harmful or explosive gases.

In an additional safety precaution, this time for foliage in the vicinity of the plant, special care has been taken to ensure that no damage is done to trees by harmful components of the exhaust gases. For this reason, the exhaust gases from the sulphuric acid unit are subjected to additional "scrubbing" and the exhaust gases from the nitric acid plant are specially treated before being discharged into the atmosphere. In addition, provisions have been made to ensure that waste waters leaving the factory do not contain any harmful materials.

There were two switch-rooms built in the ammonia plant. The 1st one was built in the ground floor of the ammonia control room. All the compressors switch gear were housed there. The 2nd one was built at the west side of the synthesis compressor building. It housed the switch gear for all the pumps on the ammonia plant.

I remember a dangerous incident when one of the underground cables going from the switch-room at the ammonia plant control room building to the 2nd switch-room at the synthesis compressor building. An underground cable failed and it tripped out the whole ammonia plant. I was on the way up the stairs to the ammonia control room when I looked out the large window on the east side of the stairwell and saw steam and water gushing up into the air from the ground. There were two cars parked at that location and they got damaged with the pressure of the gushing steam coming from the ground.

A 3rd switch-room was built on the south side of the nitric acid plant to house all the electric pumps and other items in the CAN Plants, the Acid Plants, the Bagging & Loading Plants and the Stacking Area & building.

A lot of the work done by electricians was isolating and reconnecting electric pumps, compressors and other electric equipment. We had an A4 two sheet isolation/reconnection book for that purpose.

If a process foreman wanted a pump isolated for work situation's he would call the electrician. The electrician would come to the control room as soon as he could and the process foreman would write down on the isolation request sheet, the name and number of t item of equipment he wanted isolated, and the time and date. Then he would sign the request. The electrician would fill in the acknowledgement section of the sheet by putting the name and number of the item of equipment, write the time down and date it. Then he would sign the sheet. The electrician would then go to the switch-room, isolate the said item, go back to the control room and sign the bottom section of the sheet that he has isolated the item, write down the time and date. The process foreman would then write the time, date and sign that the item is now isolated.

When the process foreman wanted the item reconnected, he would call the electrician and the opposite would take place on the second page. It is important to mention that it does not necessarily mean that the process foreman would want the item reconnected the same day. It would depend on the work being done on the item. It could even be a week before it is reconnected.

After the fatal accident occurred in the CCF Plant we brought in the system of using personal padlocks for work situations. All workers were given their personal padlock which had to be attached to the combination lock on the equipment they were working on. They would not be given a WORK PERMIT if they did not attach the padlock. When anyone was required to work on equipment that had to be electrically isolated the electrician would put his padlock on the combination lock on the switch of the electrical item. The electrician would not reconnect the item until all other padlocks were removed.

The system was used from then on and all the staff were satisfied with it for good safety reasons.

The following were the electrical and Instruments staff:

Hubert Penston   Electrical Engineer & Manager

Michael McEvoy   Electrical/Instrument Engineer

Brendan O'Reilly   Electrical/Instruments Engineer

Danny McLoughlin Electrical Foreman

Aidan O'Rourke   Electrical Foreman

Patrick O'Sullivan   Electrical Foreman

John Ahearne   Electrician

Myles Carroll   Electrician

James O'Neill   Electrician

Sean Penston   Electrician

Joseph Timmons   Electrician

Fran O'Neill   Electrician

Oliver Redmond   Electrician

Jack Bass   Electrician

Michael Shiggins Electrician

Austin Brennan   Electrical/Instruments Apprentice

Alfie Travers   Instruments forman

Callaghan Mc Carthy Senior Instruments Technician

Laurance Noctor Senior Instruments Technician

Timothy Collins Instruments Technician

Stephen Conway Instruments Technician

Martin O'Boyle Instruments Technician

As well as isolating/reconnecting electrical equipment the electricians would also be busy on checking/repairing different electric equipment including electric motors of all sizes. In plant shutdowns they would have a lot of such work in the electric workshop.

The Electrical foremen would be busy making out programs of electrical equipment and checking on their staff to make sure they were working efficiently and safely.

The Electrical/Instruments Engineers would spend a lot of their time carrying out statutory inspection on all the equipment and carrying out modifications.

The manager, Hubert Penston would be responsible for overseeing all the work and be very involved in preparing for shutdowns.

The Instruments technicians would also have very valuable work to do. Every plant would need, in their control room, temperatures, pressures, levels etc on the instruments, fitted in a way that they could be easily read for plant control. The Instrument technicians would check that the readings on the plant reactors, vessels, tanks etc. were correctly installed and transmitted to the control rooms panels for efficient operation.

CHAPTER 10

PERSONNEL DEPARTMENT

Jack Martin

	SURNAME	FIRST NAME	AREA	SECTION	CATEGORY
001	Carroll	Kevin	Finance	Accounts	Admin Supervisor
002	Young	Donal	Finance	Accounts	Admin Supervisor
003	Kelly	Thomas	Finance	Accounts	Clerical
004	Porter	John	Finance	Accounts	Factory Accountant
005	Duane	Brian	Finance	Accounts	Snr Clerical
006	Hagan	William	Finance	Accounts	Snr Clerical
007	Bannon	Marina	Payroll	Accounts	
008	Byrne	Bridget	Personnel	Admin Welfare	Cleaner
009	Byrne	Andrew	Production	B&L	Shift Operator
010	Carey	Liam	Production	B&L	Shift Operator
011	Cullen	Patrick	Production	B&L	Shift Operator
012	Curran	David	Production	B&L	Shift Operator
013	Doyle	Thomas	Production	B&L	Shift Operator
014	Fox	Terry	Production	B&L	Shift Operator
015	Halford	William	Production	B&L	Shift Operator
016	Hannigan	Paul	Production	B&L	Shift Operator
017	Hayden	Derek	Temp	B&L	Shift Operator
018	Howard	Brian	Production	B&L	Shift Operator
019	Kealy	Tony	Production	B&L	Shift Operator
020	Kenny	David	Production	B&L	Shift Operator
021	Keogh	William	Production	B&L	Shift Operator
022	Kinch	Niall	Production	B&L	Shift Operator
023	Lynch	Peter	Production	B&L	Shift Operator
024	Murphy	David	Production	B&L	Shift Operator
025	Mythen	Desmond	Production	B&L	Shift Operator
026	Redmond	James	Production	B&L	Shift Operator
027	Townsend	Tommy	Production	B&L	Shift Operator

028	Weadick	Daragh	Production	B&L	Shift Operator
029	Whelan	William	Production	B&L	Shift Operator
030	Wolohan	Adam	Temp	B&L	Shift Operator
031	Wolohan	Henry	Production	B&L	Shift Operator
032	Balfe	James	Production	B&L	Snr Shift Operator
033	Doyle	Michael	Production	B&L	Snr Shift Operator
034	Gannon	Michael	Production	B&L	Snr Shift Operator
035	Shanley	Seamus	Production	B&L	Snr Shift Operator
036	Keenan	Donal	Production	CAN	Engineer
037	Cullen	Seamus	Temp	CAN	General Operative
038	Bardon	Paul	Production	CAN	Shift Operator
039	Byrne	Myles	Production	CAN	Shift Operator
040	Byrne	William J.	Production	CAN	Shift Operator
041	Campbell	Michael	Production	CAN	Shift Operator
042	Carton	Michael	Production	CAN	Shift Operator
043	Conway	Andrew	Production	CAN	Shift Operator
044	Doyle	Michael	Production	CAN	Shift Operator
045	Fitzgerald	Denis	Production	CAN	Shift Operator
046	Gannon	Pat	Production	CAN	Shift Operator
047	Hannigan	Sean	Production	CAN	Shift Operator
048	Heeney	Shane	Production	CAN	Shift Operator
049	Howard	Timothy	Production	CAN	Shift Operator
050	Kavanagh	James	Production	CAN	Shift Operator
051	Keenan	John	Production	CAN	Shift Operator
052	Lott	David	Production	CAN	Shift Operator
053	Martin	Thomas	Production	CAN	Shift Operator
054	McQuillan	Ian	Production	CAN	Shift Operator
055	Murphy	Matthew	Production	CAN	Shift Operator
056	Murphy	Seamus	Production	CAN	Shift Operator
057	O'Leary	Patrick	Production	CAN	Shift Operator
058	Porter	Darrell	Production	CAN	Shift Operator
059	Redmond	Frank	Production	CAN	Shift Operator

060	Shelton	Joseph	Production	CAN	Shift Operator
061	Weadick	Joe Jnr	Production	CAN	Shift Operator
062	Whitty	Edward	Production	CAN	Shift Operator
063	Wixted	Eugene	Production	CAN	Shift Operator
064	Donegan	Noel	Production	CAN	Snr Shift Operator
065	Lambert	Michael	Production	CAN	Snr Shift Operator
066	Molloy	Michael / Milo	Production	CAN	Snr Shift Operator
067	Monaghan	Patrick	Production	CAN	Snr Shift Operator
068	O'Reilly	William	Production	CAN	Snr Shift Operator
069	O'Sullivan	Trevor	Engineering	Civil	Engineer
070	Clancy	George	Production	Day Foreman	Foreman
071	Scallan	Eamonn	Production	Day Foreman	Foreman
072	Hore	Daniel	Engineering	Drawing Office	Admin Supervisor
073	McDonagh	Paul	Engineering	Drawing Office	Senior Draughtsma
074	Brennan	Austin	Engineering	Elect & Insts	Apprentice
075	Aherne	Michael John	Engineering	Electrical	Electrician
076	Carroll	Myles	Engineering	Electrical	Electrician
077	O'Neill	James	Engineering	Electrical	Electrician
078	Penston	Sean	Engineering	Electrical	Electrician
079	O'Sullivan	Patrick	Engineering	Electrical	Foreman
080	Timmons	Joseph	PHI	Electrician	Electrician
081	Wheston	Stephen	Factory Services	Env Chemist	Engineer
082	Flood	William	Factory Services	Factory Manager	Management
083	Brennan	John	Engineering	Fitter	Fitter
084	Brennan	Paul	Engineering	Fitter	Fitter
085	Byrne	Thomas	Engineering	Fitter	Fitter
086	Carroll	Peter	Engineering	Fitter	Fitter
087	Connors	Thomas	PHI	Fitter	Fitter
088	Curran	Matthew	Engineering	Fitter	Fitter
089	Curran	Thomas / Joe	Engineering	Fitter	Fitter
090	Deithrick	Gerard	Engineering	Fitter	Fitter
091	Dowling	Alfred	Engineering	Fitter	Fitter

092	Doyle	Brian	Engineering	Fitter	Fitter
093	Doyle	John	Engineering	Fitter	Fitter
094	Driver	Thomas	Engineering	Fitter	Fitter
095	Kinch	Matthew	Engineering	Fitter	Fitter
096	Lacey	John	Engineering	Fitter	Fitter
097	Murray	Thomas	Engineering	Fitter	Fitter
098	O'Leary	Brendan	Engineering	Fitter	Fitter
099	O'Sullivan	Murtagh	Engineering	Fitter	Fitter
100	Prestage	George	Engineering	Fitter	Fitter
101	Doyle	Kevin	PHI	Fitter	Fitter
102	Masterson	Nicholas	PHI	Fitter	Fitter
103	Walker	William	PHI	Fitter	Fitter
104	Riley	Brendan	Engineering	Inst / Electrical	Engineer
105	Klaasen	Eric	Engineering	Inst Technologist	Engineer
106	Walker	Raymond	Engineering	Inst Technologist (S)	Instrument Tech'n
107	Travers	Alfie	Engineering	Instruments	Foreman
108	Collins	Timothy	Engineering	Instruments	Instrument Tech'n
109	Conway	Stephen	Engineering	Instruments	Instrument Tech'n
110	O'Boyle	Martin	Engineering	Instruments	Instrument Tech'n
111	McCarthy	Callaghan	Engineering	Instruments	Snr Inst Tech'n
112	Noctor	Laurence	Engineering	Instruments	Snr Inst Tech'n
113	Cashman	Anthony	Production	Lab	Shift Operator
114	Cuffe	Kenneth	Production	Lab	Shift Operator
115	Darcy	Michael	Production	Lab	Shift Operator
116	Mc Cormack	Conor	Production	Lab	Shift Operator
117	Morris	David	Production	Lab	Shift Operator
118	Fanning	Michael	Production	Lab	Snr lab techn
119	Furlong	Annette	Factory Services	Loss Control Co-Ordinator	Snr Clerical
120	Phillips	Paddy	PHI	Fitter Craftsman	Fitter
121	Kavanagh	Conal	Personnel	Manager	Management
122	Collins	William	Apprentice	Mech	Apprentice
123	Alexander	Brian	Engineering	Mechanical	Foreman

124	Mulhall	Thomas	Engineering	Mechanical	Foreman
125	O'Brien	Paddy	Engineering	Mechanical	Foreman
126	Watters	Thomas	Engineering	Mechanical	Foreman
127	Blake	Vincent	Engineering	Mechanical	Foreman
128	Whitty	Mary	Personnel	Medical	On - Call Nurse
129	Hannigan	Denis	Production	NA	Shift Operator
130	Hynes	Thomas	Production	NA	Shift Operator
131	Ivory	Joseph	Production	NA	Shift Operator
132	Kavanagh	John	Production	NA	Shift Operator
133	Kinsella	John	Production	NA	Shift Operator
134	Lambert	Michael	Production	NA	Shift Operator
135	Murphy	Nicholas	Production	NA	Shift Operator
136	Hughes	James	Production	NA	Snr Shift Operator
137	Power	Patrick	Production	NA	Snr Shift Operator
138	Travers	Peter	Production	NA	Snr Shift Operator
139	Tyrrell	James	Production	NA	Snr Shift Operator
140	Redmond	Angela	Personnel	Night Cleaner	General Operative
141	O'Shaughnessy	Ann	Personnel	OHS Officer	Management
142	Carty	Jean	Personnel	Surgery	
143	Murray	Esther	Personnel	Surgery	
144	Whelan	Peter	Engineering	Operations	Management
145	Martin	John	Personnel	Personnel & Training	Management
146	Cleary	Brian	Engineering	Planning & Inspection	Engineer
147	McCaughey	Anthony	Engineering	Plant	Engineer
148	Phelan	James	Engineering	Plant Engineer	Engineer
149	Doyle	Rodney	Engineering	Plant Engineer CAN	Engineer
150	Allman	Alexander	Personnel	Postage & Stationery	Clerical
151	Ryan	Patrick	Production	Process & Projects	Engineer
152	Furlong	James	PHI	Process Day Foreman	Process Day Foreman
153	Spacey	Terrence	Production	Production Services	Engineer
154	Crotty	Patrick	Engineering	Projects & Stores	Engineer

155	Nolan	Damien	Engineering	Purchasing & Stores	Admin Supervisor
156	Quirke	Mary	Personnel	Reception	Clerical
157	Weadick	Joseph	Factory Services	Safety	Management
158	McNamara	James	Dublin	Safety & Environment Mgr	Management
159	Moriarty	Emer	Personnel	Secretarial	Clerical
160	Brennan	James	Engineering	Semi - Skilled	General Operative
161	Byrne	Tony	Engineering	Semi - Skilled	General Operative
162	Collins	Thomas	Engineering	Semi - Skilled	General Operative
163	Conroy	James	Engineering	Semi - Skilled	General Operative
164	Hunt	Frank	Engineering	Semi - Skilled	General Operative
165	Kavanagh	James William	PHI	Semi - Skilled	General Operative
166	Sheridan	Thomas	Engineering	Semi - Skilled	General Operative
167	Byrne	John	Production	Senior Shift Op	Snr Shift Operator
168	McEvoy	Michael	Factory Services	SHE	Management
169	Byrne	Michael	Production	Shift Foreman	Foreman
170	Kealy	John	Production	Shift Foreman	Foreman
171	Kealy	Noel	Production	Shift Foreman	Foreman
172	O'Sullivan	John	Production	Shift Foreman	Foreman
173	Redmond	Paul	Production	Shift Foreman	Foreman
174	Cullen	James	PHI	Shift Operator	Shift Operator
175	Finn	Paddy	PHI	Shift Operator	Shift Operator
176	O'Reilly	Paddy	PHI	Shift Operator	Shift Operator
177	Cullen	John	PHI	Shift Operator Weighbridge & Security	Shift Operator
178	Kavanagh	William	Personnel	Site Welfare	General Operative
179	Byrne	Rhoda	Engineering	Snr Clerical	Snr Clerical
180	Forde	Noel	PHI	Snr Shift Operator	Snr Shift Operator
181	Byrne	Michael	Production	Stacking	Day Operator
182	Chambers	Anthony	Production	Stacking	Day Operator
183	Doyle	Michael	Production	Stacking	Day Operator
184	Kennedy	Patrick	Production	Stacking	Day Operator

185	Osborne	John	Production	Stacking	Day Operator
186	Kinch	Michael	Production	Stacking	Snr Day Operator
187	Donohue	Harry	Engineering	Stores	Day Operator
188	Doyle	Thomas	Engineering	Stores	Day Operator
189	O'Rourke	Kieran	Engineering	Stores	Day Operator
190	O'Loughlin	William	Production	Utilities & RMI	Engineer
191	Holden	Michael	Production	Utilities & RMI	Shift Operator
192	Morris	Nicholas	Production	Utilities & RMI	Shift Operator
193	O'Toole	Anthony	Production	Utilities & RMI	Shift Operator
194	Price	Richard Jnr	Production	Utilities & RMI	Shift Operator
195	Byrne	Michael / Joe	Production	Utilities & RMI	Snr Shift Operator
196	Carley	John	Production	Utilities & RMI	Snr Shift Operator
197	Craine	Thomas	Production	Utilities & RMI	Snr Shift Operator
198	Kealy	William	Production	Utilities & RMI	Snr Shift Operator
199	Keegan	Joe Keegan	Production	Utilities & RMI	Snr Shift Operator
200	Keegan	Peter	Production	Utilities & RMI	Snr Shift Operator
201	Keenan	Liam	Production	Utilities & RMI	Snr Shift Operator
202	Nicholson	Michael	Production	Utilities & RMI	Snr Shift Operator
203	O'Loughlin	Sean	Production	Utilities & RMI	Snr Shift Operator
204	Pierce	Thomas	Production	Utilities & RMI	Snr Shift Operator
205	Shortle	Joseph	Production	Utilities & RMI	Snr Shift Operator
206	Healy	James	Factory Services	Weighbridge / Security	Shift Operator
207	Lawler	Seamus	Factory Services	Weighbridge / Security	Shift Operator
208	O'Dare	Jack	Factory Services	Weighbridge / Security	Shift Operator
209	Dempsey	James	Factory Services	Weighbridge / Security	Snr Shift Operator
210	O'Leary	Michael	Apprentice		Apprentice
211	O'Reilly	Pascal	Apprentice		Apprentice
212	O'Shea	Andrew	Apprentice		Apprentice
213	Ward	Daniel	Apprentice		Apprentice
214	Doyle	Owen	CSU & Logistics		Management

215	Fitzgerald	Patrick	CSU & Logistics Manager		Management
216	O'Toole	John	Data Processing		Management
217	Kearon	James	DP		Snr Clerical
218	Mc Geary	Christopher	CSU		Snr Clerical
219	Redmond	Martin	CSU		Snr Clerical
220	Thornton	Timothy	CSU		Snr Clerical
221	O'Reilly	Brian	DP		
222	O'Rourke	Denis	DP		
223	Furlong	Jim	Process Day Foreman		
224	Kavanagh	Betty	On - Call Nurse		

The above staff were in the company when we went into Liquation in October 2002. The list was accumulated by Jack Martin, Personnel Officer.

CHAPTER 11

PURCHASING & STORES

Damien Nolan

Purchasing and Stores Arklow (NET – IFI Arklow)

Nítrigin Éireann Teoranta (NET) later to become Irish Fertilizer Industries (IFI) started production in Arklow in 1965. At the time it was one of, if not, the largest chemical industries in Ireland and for that reason it required a first-class Purchasing Department and also a first-class Stores/Warehouse Department to control both spending and stock.

At the start of production there was a separate Purchasing Department and Stores Department.

Both departments were situated in the same building which was attached to the stores. The Purchasing Department was on the top floor and the Stores administration staff were on the bottom floor. The storemen and fork-truck drivers were situated in the main stores. There was also a Tool Crib attached to the stores, this was for storing specialised tools that would be used and then returned for late use. The stores had its own locker-room and small canteen. This facility was at the bottom end of the site close to the back gate which was very handy for deliveries as suppliers did not have to travel the full length of the site and it also cut out the need for some of the trucks travelling through the town of Arklow.

Each department had its own separate manager, supervisors and clerical staff, the stores had its own foreman, storemen and fork-truck drivers.

In order to come in line with industrial best practice it was decided to amalgamate the purchasing and stores departments under one manager and for them to become the one department called Purchasing/Stores. This meant that staff were free to work in either department and decisions that would effect both departments could be made by one manager.

Over time new production plants were built and with each new plant came the need for new spare parts. The original stores was not big enough to cater for all these new spares so a new warehouse was built beside the stores, this new warehouse became known as the extension and was mainly used for storing large items that could not be stored outside. Large items that could be stored outside were kept in one of the compounds.

The Purchasing and Stores Departments had developed a nine-step process which was from the time an item/service was required to the time the order was complete. (1) Recognise the need. (2) Raise the requisition. (3) Select the suppliers. (4)Negotiate with suppliers. (5) Raise the order. (6) Monitor/Expedite the order. (7) Receive the goods/service. (8) Approve the invoice. (9) File completed orders.

When the Purchasing and Stores departments first started they used a paper based system. Every purchase requisition and stores requisition had to be hand written. The information on the purchase requisition was used to order items from suppliers and the information on the stores requisition was used to take items out of stock for use around the site.

In the early days of NET starting the stores was staffed 24 hours a day seven days a week. Some, but not all, of the storemen were on shift work. One storeman would be on duty in the stores outside normal working hours in order to supply material if required. Later, because of voluntary redundancy, it was decided to do away with shift work in the stores and introduce "On Call".

This was where a member of the staff could be called upon to come into work at any time of the day or night to locate an item that was urgently required. The person on call would be required to cover for one week. At first every on call staff member would be required to do one week in six. However, after many rounds of redundancies this ended with only one person being on call all the time.

One unlucky person who was on call during the installation and commissioning of a new plant was called in to work on Christmas Eve, Christmas Day and Saint Stephens Day. This was a very rare and unusual occurrence.

The stores kept thousands of different items in stock and each item had its own separate card on a kardex system. Every transaction, purchase requisition, purchase order, goods received note, stores requisition and stores return note, had to be recorded manually on the system. As the number of stock items increased so did the amount of transactions that had to be manually recorded. This lead to delays in keeping stock records up to date and stock records that are not up to date are useless.

It was at this stage that the decision was made to computerise the purchasing and stores function.

The computer system was written in house by members of the computer department with input from the purchasing and stores staff. Staff in both departments received training on how the new system would work. When the computer system was written and tested every record had to be transferred over from the manual kardex system to the new computer system. Both systems had to run side by side for a month in order to ensure that the new system was working correctly and that the stock balances on both systems were the same. Not all of the functions however were computerised. Requisitions, return notes, purchase requisitions and GRN's (Goods Received Notes) were hand written and the information had to be punched into the computer so that the system could keep control of stock and produce purchase orders.

There were two types of purchase orders used by the Purchasing Department, one was a stock order used for buying items that were kept in stock and that had reached their reorder point, the other was a direct issue order and this was used to purchase items that were not kept in stock and were issued directly to the person who raised the requisition.

Most of the items kept in stock were used in the maintenance of plant and equipment. Bulky Raw Materials were not kept in the stores. Raw Materials were purchased central by the head office in Dublin.

As mentioned earlier there were thousands of different items kept in stock. Each SKU (stock keeping unit) had its own individual code number, each code number was made up of seven numbers this meant that the system could cater for different items. For example, the code number for disposable cotton glover was 47 22 101. Each SKU also had its own location address (where it was kept and could be located). For example an item that was kept in the extension the location code would start with Ext. and then the rack number and then the shelf number. Each SKU could have from one to thousands in stock. For example, a spare turbine could have a stock balance of one, or protective disposable gloves could have a stock balance of thousands.

Most of the original plant and equipment came from Germany and for this reason a large proportion of spares had to be ordered from Germany. Most of these spares were based on the metric system. For this reason there appeared to be a duplication of some stock items, for example, a 1/2" bolt is very similar to a 12 mm bolt but you can't put a 12mm nut on a 1/2" bolt. Sometimes this was very hard to explain to external auditors at stock taking time which was carried out once a year. The physical stock take would take the best part of a week with several teams of counters made up of one from accounts and one from purchasing/stores. One to count and one to record.

Apart from Raw Materials every item and service used in the factory had to be purchased by the Purchasing Department and every item that cane into the factory had to come into the Goods Inwards Department which was part of the stores. When a delivery came into Goods Inwards it was unloaded by the fork-truck driver or taken in by the storemen. Every delivery was inspected by the storemen and signed for. If the delivery docked did not quote an official order the storeman would refuse to sign it and call for one of the stores clerical staff to check it out and see if they could find an order no. (This was before the stores was computerised, because after computerisation the storeman could check the computer system themself and see if they could locate an order number based on the suppliers outstanding orders).

When the docket was signed it was passed on to the clerical staff in Goods Inwards who would register it in the Goods Inwards Daybook and give it a unique number this number would be written on the delivery docket and the docket would be attached to a copy of the order, this would be given to the storeman who would make the delivery with the same number. This documentation would be placed at the bottom of a tray and the storeman would inspect the delivery at a later stage depending on the number of deliveries to be inspected. There was great flexibility among the storemen and if the item was required it would be given priority and inspected and cleared immediately.

(Purchasing and Stores staff were aware that if an item was required to keep equipment operating it was their responsibility to get it to the end user as soon as possible.)

When it came time to inspect the delivery the storeman would get the documentation and check the entry number and then inspect the delivery with the corresponding number. As mentioned earlier some orders were for stock items and some orders were for items that would be used directly on the plant. The items were inspected and compared to the description on the order, if everything was in order the items would be cleared for use. If they were stock items each item would be marked with its corresponding stock code and placed in its correct location. If it was a direct issue item it would be marked with the order number and either delivered to the plant or left in a designated area for collection.

When the delivery was cleared the paperwork would be returned to the Goods Inwards clerical staff and they would prepare a Good Received Note (GRN) this was used for updating the kardex or later the computer system. A copy of the GRN was also sent to the Invoice Clarence section of the Accounts Department it was used as versification that the goods were received and allowed the invoice to be cleared and the supplier paid the paperwork was then sent to the Purchasing Department to be filed behind the order. The order would then be filed as complete if all the items were received, if not it would be placed in the outstanding/pending file.

On one occasion a delivery of a gearbox was received from a German supplier. When the wooden crate was opened it was noticed that the gearbox was packed in straw. It was also noted that the straw was infected with fleas. Immediately the fork-truck driver moved the wooden crate to a remote area in the extension and sealed off the area with safety tape and informed the stores supervisor. The local pest control company was called in and the infestation was quickly cleared up and the straw removed. A new clause was added to the terms and conditions on the back of the purchase orders," No Straw To Be Used As Packing".

The delivery service available in the 60's 70' and 80' was not as good as it is now. A delivery from Germany could take weeks and from the UK could take days. Next day delivery from Ireland would depend on the time the order was placed, if it was placed in the afternoon you might not get it the next day.

Because of the long delivery time from Germany every effort was made by the Purchasing Department to locate manufacturers in Ireland or the UK who could supply the necessary spare parts. Drawings of spare parts were prepared by the skilled Draughtsmen in the Drawing Department. When a spare part was required Purchasing would send out a request for a quotation accompanied by a drawing to manufacturers in Ireland and the UK (Irish manufacturers – especially local ones -were given preference, based on quality and price, because of the delivery time involved). Many Irish companies were used to manufacture and supply spare parts that heretofore had to come from Germany. However, many items still had to be purchased from Germany and the UK.

As mentioned earlier deliveries from the UK could take days and this would be extended if the weekend was involved. On several occasions purchasing or stores staff would be asked to go to the UK by car on the next available ferry drive to a particular company and pick up an urgently required spare part then get the next available ferry back to Ireland and bring the part to the site. As the plants were operation 24 hours a day seven days a week any loss in production could not be regained by working overtime. The expense of doing this far outweighed the value of lost production.

Many of the suppliers used by NET/IFI were based in Dublin. In order to speed up deliveries and cut down on delivery costs local courier companies were contracted to go to Dublin one or two days a week and collect parts that were ordered. Suppliers were asked to contact Purchasing and inform them when items were ready for collection and not to send them out. Purchasing would prepare a list of suppliers and give it to the local courier who would collect the parts and deliver them that evening if required, if not the next morning.

On one occasion conveyor belt rollers were required urgently and no drawing was available. A new supplier was asked if they could manufacture and supply these rollers urgently, they said that they could

65

manufacture and supply within 48 hours but that they would need a drawing. When they were told there was no drawing available they said that they could make them if they got a sample. A sample was sent to them and they came back to purchasing with a price. A purchase order was produced and a copy was sent by fax. The order stated, "please supply 20 rollers exactly as per sample". Unfortunately the roller was a used worn one, the sprocket on one side was worn more than the one on the other side and the roller itself tapered at one end. The supplier was true to his word. The 20 rollers arrived within 48 hours exactly as per the worn sample, worn and tapered at one end. A drawing was prepared and the same supplier was given the repeat order, after all it was no fault of his. They became a regular supplier of rollers as their work and prices were excellent.

Hundreds of stock items were used on site every day. In order to get an item out of stock a stores requisition had to be prepared and signed by a foreman or higher and then presented to the storeman at the counter. When the requisition was received it would be inspected by the storeman to make sure it had a valid Cost Code (where the spare parts were to be debited to), had the proper signature and also had the correct code numbers. If the items were large and had to be delivered by fork-truck then the storeman would check on a delivery location. If the items were small the storeman would check the system to see if the items were in stock and what was their location. If the items were in stock he would get them and give them to the person at the counter. If the items were large he would give the requisition to the fork truck driver and he would get the items and deliver them to the required area on site. When the requisition was completed it was given to the clerical staff who would then update the system, if the stock had reached its reorder point they would inform the Purchasing Department. The requisitions were then sent to the Accounts Department who would use them to debit the budget for the plant they were used on, based on the Cost Code provided. This was to show how much it was costing to run each plant and each individual piece of machinery.

When new apprentices first started to work on site they were often sent to the stores with stores requisition to collect items. On some occasions, as a bit of fun by the older members of staff, they would be sent to collect items that did not exist, for example a glass hammer or a left hander screwdriver. Sometimes they would be sent down and told to ask for a "long weight" but what they ended up getting was a "long wait". The storeman would tell them he would have to go and look for it. Eventually he would come back and ask them "well, did you have a long wait"? He usually told them "your not the first and you wont be the last". Most of them took it with good grace and went back to work.

Sometimes items were taken out of stock but for various reason they would not be used on the plant. These items were then returned to the stores and placed back into stock. It was a reverse procedure to requesting items from stock. A stores return note would be prepared usually by the person who requested the item. A cost code, stock number and quantity to be returned would be entered onto the return note and then signed. This would accompany the goods back to the stores. The storeman would then place the goods back into their location and the return note would be given to the clerical staff so the records could be updated. Purchasing were also informed about the return in case they might be going to reorder the item. The return note would be sent to the Accounts Department so that the plant could receive credit for the value of the item returned.

Every stock item had a reorder point and a reorder quantity, they were based on price, usage and delivery time. The value of the stock item was calculated using weighted average price.

If the stock balance of an item went below its reorder point purchasing would be informed. They would have to do a calculation to determine how many to order. For example, if the reorder point was 5 and the reorder quantity was 10 and the quantity in stock was 2 then they would place an order for 13 (reorder point + reorder quantity – quantity in stock). However, some items came in packs and adjustments to the order quantity would have to be made. For example, gloves came in packs of a dozen pairs but they were issued from stock in single pairs.

Purchasing had the responsibility for getting the best value for money spent, bearing in mind quality and delivery time and cost of delivery. As mentioned earlier there weree two different types of orders, stock orders and direct issue orders, but the same procedure was followed for each. When a stock item reached its reorder point purchasing would be informed. If an item was required that was not held in stock a purchase requisition would be raised by the person requiring the item and this requisition would be sent to the purchasing department.

Purchasing would examine each item or service that was required and then locate suppliers who could supply the part or service. Every effort was made to find three suppliers for each item and service.

Requests for Quotation would be prepared and sent to the three selected suppliers looking for price and availability. A date by which the quotation was to be received by the Purchasing Department was also stated, this was dictated by the urgency of the item or service.

When the quotations were received, they would be examined and a decision would be made as to who the order would be placed with, it was not always the supplier with the lowest price who received the order but the one who offered the best service based on price, quality, delivery time and cost of delivery.

In the early stages orders were either typed or in some cases hand written. With computerisation they were all produced by the computer directly from the requisitions.

All of the orders were sent out by post and suppliers were requested to acknowledge that they had received the order. If they did not acknowledge that they had received the order they would be contacted by phone to verify that they would or would not supply the items on the order. In some cases orders were phoned or faxed to the supplier, depending on how urgent the items were, a follow-up order would be sent by post marked "Confirmation of phone/fax order".

Every item on an order would have a full description, (the stock number if it was a stock item), the quantity required, the quoted price and the date the item was required.

Outstanding orders would be examined on a regular basis to see if the required delivery date had not been met. If the items were not received on time the supplier would be contacted and asked to explain the reason for the delay in delivery. Depending on the answer the order would be cancelled and reordered with another supplier, or an extended delivery date would be accepted. Critical orders would be examined several timed between the date of placing the order and the expected delivery date and a progress report would be prepared. The supplier of these orders would be contacted and asked how the order was proceeding and if the required delivery date would be achieved or not. If for some reason the delivery date could not be met the relevant department would be informed in case planned maintenance dates needed to be changed.

In the mid 1990's it was decided to purchase a new Purchasing and Stores Computer System which was to be linked to the Maintenance System. The new system was called PEMAC and it was supplied and installed by a company called PMI.

This new computer system did away with most of the paper work involved in Purchasing and Stores. Orders were still printed as most suppliers still required a physical order.

Stores requisition, return notes, purchase requisitions and GRN's were all completed on the computer system. The old computer system needed to be updated every night, this meant that the stock balances on the computer were not accurate. If an item was taken out of stock first thing in the morning the system would not show the transaction until the next day.

However, with the new PEMAC system, transactions were update immediately they happened which lead to a more accurate stock control system.

As mentioned before the stores held thousands of different stock items which ranged from Abrasive wheels to Zinc plates and many more in between. (Bearings, Chemicals, Drums, Electrical cable, Fire Extinguishers, Gas cylinders. Helmets, Instrumentation, Jointing compound, Knives, Lighting, Molybdenum, Nuts, Oxygen Tanks, Pipes, Quartz sand, Rollers, Stainless Steel, Telephones, Universal Joints, Vehicle parts, Washers, X- ray Equipment, Yale locks).

Just to finish off with a list of some, but not all, of the people who worked in the Purchasing and Stores departments over the years. A special thanks goes to Peter Mills, who worked in the Purchasing Department, for supplying most of these names.

Kevin Carroll, Jim Dempsey, Joe Duffy, Jimmy Esmonde, Martin Fitzgerald, Annette Furlong, Dermot Green, Sean Hennessey, Tony Hobbs, Mary Carmel Horan, Jim Kavanagh,

Gerry Kavanagh, Joe Keegan, Pamela Lott, Bruce McDonagh, Sil McDoward, Chris McGeary,

Peter Mills, Liam Moran, Jack Morris, Tommy O'Brien, Al O'Connor, Sean O'Reilly, John Owens, Tommy Pierce, Tommy Redmond, Dorothy Rees, Fonsie Sheils, Patricia Sinnott, Pat Spencer, Phil Vaneesbeck.

When IFI closed in 2002 there was only five people left working in the Stores and Purchasing Department, they were Rhoda Byrne, Harry Donohue, Tommy Doyle, Kieran O'Rourke and Damien Nolan

Purchasing and Stores Arklow (NET – IFI Arklow)

CHAPTER 12

LABORATORY

Terry Spacey

Laboratory

The laboratory was housed in a single-story building, located in the center of the site, adjacent to all the production plants. It was managed initially by the Chief Chemist but in later years by the Section Manager Services. It was manned by both day and shift technicians providing 24hr cover.

The main function of the laboratory was to provide Quality Control in various sections of the operation by monitoring the production processes through sampling and analysis at different stages to achieve good process control, and ensure products meet specification. This required the analysis of various streams including gases, liquids and solids.

To produce a quality product any raw materials used in the process had to be analyzed to confirm, or otherwise, that they conformed to specification.

The main raw materials used in the production processes during the operation at the Arklow site included the following:

Limestone -Calcium and magnesium carbonates sourced from Jikljennt and north Dublin, used in the production of Calcium ammonium nitrate 27.5%N CAN Fertilizer.

Phosphate rock – imported from Morocco for the production of phosphoric acid, which was a feedstock in the chemical production of compound, NPK fertilizer. This was discontinued with the closure of the acid plant in 1981.

Diammonium Phosphate DAP – (18%N.20%P) – imported in granular form for the Bulk Blending of a range of NPK compound products

Potash -Potassium Chloride (50%K)–also imported in granular form from Cheshire, England for the producing of NPK products By Bulk Blending

Note: The Bulk Blending process for producing NPK compounds was the mixing of CAN, DAO and Potash in the correct ratios to produce the desired compound fertilizer e. g. 10%N -10%P-20%K or 18%N-6P-12%K

The main products being produced during the operation of the Arklow site were:

ACID PRODUCTION

Sulfuric acid

Phosphoric acid

Nitric acids

Ammonia, produced in Arklow until 1981. From there on it was produced in Marino Point, Cork.

FERTILIZER PRODUCTION

Ammonium Sulphate (NH4)2SO4

Calcium Ammonium Nitrate (CAN) 27.5%N- Granular and Prill products.

Complete Compound Fertilizers (CCF)- NPK production, initially by chemical process but latterly by Bulk Blending of raw materials- CAN + Potash + Diammonium phosphate.

Fertilizer products sold in both Irish and European markets needed to comply with 'The European Marketing of Fertilizer Products Regulations'

Regular checks of these products were carried out by Inspectors from the Department of Agriculture to ensure compliance with the regulations.

Services

In addition to the above the laboratory was required to monitor other areas such as:

The water systems including soft water, boiler feed and circulating waters of KM KM steam raising boilers.

The sampling and analysis of the final effluent discharged into the Avoca River as required by the Environment Protection Agency EPA.

The testing of packaging materials e.g. polythene sacks and pallet hoods used for protection of products during storage on site.

Non-routine analysis as requested by plant personnel for the investigation of any process problems.

The laboratory was suitably equipped to meet the requirements of a complex chemical production site.

CHAPTER 13

ROASTER PLANT

Sean Grehan

Sean Grehan joined NET as an operator in August 1971 in preparation for the opening of the 2100 Roaster Plant. They had a team of four persons join at the same time. The Roaster was only being built so they began training on the 1100 plant.

The 1100 plant was manufacturing sulphuric acid for use on the other plants and some was sold. This plant used imported sulphur as the raw material. Sulphur was burned to produce SO_2 gas. This gas was put through a converter when an extra oxygen molecule was added to convert it into SO3. This SO3 was then absorbed into water (H_2O). H_2O + SO3 equals H_2SO_4 (sulphuric acid).

The principal user of sulphuric acid on site was the Phosphoric Acid Plant. In this plant the sulphuric acid reacted with GNAP (Ground North African Phosphate) which was imported from Morocco. This reaction produced Phosphoric Acid (H3PO4) and a Bi-Product known as Gypsum.

The Phosphoric Acid was utilised on the CCF (complete compound fertiliser) Plant to supply the phosphorus element of the NPK Fertiliser. The gypsum was initially waste and was pumped out in the marsh. Later it was pumped out to sea and finally it was the main raw material for the Gypsum Factory on the north Quay Arklow. Named the 'Wallboard Factory.

Sulphuric Acid was also used on site for the 1200 Plant which made Sulphate of Ammonia Fertiliser. It was also sold to the Mining Industry. Sulphuric Acid was sent to the Avoca Mines and Tara Mines in Navan to name but a few.

The Roaster Plant was designed to burn Iron Pyrites at a very high temperature (1800 deg.c.). Iron Pyrites was a waste product from the Avoca Mines and was difficult to store. Many fields in the river valley contained "Ponds" of it. The Pyrites contained, amongst other elements - sulphur. This means that NET no longer needed to import sulphur from Spain.

The Pyrites needed very high temperatures to burn. The Roaster "Oven" needed oil to heat the floating Bed. Air pressure applied underneath raised the bed above the oven floor and oil burners heated the raised bed of cinders.

When the temperature was sufficiently high, raw pyrites was fed in and burned. The burned pyrites produced Co_2 and Cinder in combination. The Cinder was extracted in a number of cyclones and the SO_2 gas was sent to the 1100 Plant to manufacture the Sulphuric Acid.

The Cinder extracted was transferred by conveyor to the Cinder Storage Shed. Cinder was a very fine red dust and had to be watered to be stored. Truck loads were transported regularly to the Roadstone

Facility at Arklow Rock. It was sold to the Roadstone Company for making Red Roads and running tracks and was also sold to Companies in Britain for the same reason.

CHAPTER 14

DRAWING OFFICE

Danny Hore

Nitrogen Eireann Teo – Irish Fertilizers Industries from 1974 to 2002

ENGINEERING DRAWING OFFICE

In 1974 the drawing office staff consisted of one chief draughtsman, two supervisors, ten draughtsmen and one office secretary.

The office was divided into two groups of five draughtsmen, one group for each supervisor to facilitate the different types of engineers with design and fabrication drawings for their various production plants.

The drawing office was always busy in those days and very facilitating to all managers and engineers when they put in a job request for a draughtman to do whatever they required drawings, for a design arrangement or a single component drawing to be manufactured in our site fabrication workshop. From time to time we would outsource the fabrication drawings to local fabrication workshops to help meet the demands of plant shutdowns schedules.

Those early days in the drawing office we were using the metric measure system on all drawings because machinery on site was designed by a company called Lurgi who were a German company.

We used adjustable height drawing boards and tracing paper to produce drawings, using lead pencils and rotring rapidograph ink pens which gave a more presentable drawing.

All drawings were done to metric standard, namely DIN Standard's which were new to many of us at the time, because many of us in the drawing office at that time would have had previously only used the imperial system of feet and inches and fractions of an inch. The metric system was more acceptable when working on mechanical drawings because you were working in meters and millimeters.

This system of using drawing boards to produce drawings became obsolete in around 1990 with the introduction of AutoCad version11 which didn't take us that long to adjust to doing drawings on a monitor and print out your finished drawings using an inkjet plotter. This new technology was a big plus and time saving when producing drawings from the way it was in the earlier days of producing drawings.

I always remembered what my manager had said to me when I told him it would cost in the region of £40,000 for two AutoCad work stations in our office and he replied I will get back to you, I asked what reason had he got for not been satisfied on the cost, his answer was, I have forty good reasons. It was really a good investment.

Over the years that followed the drawing office personnel was no stranger to redundancies where we suffered the loss of many good experienced draughts-men.

I would say without hesitation that I really am grateful for having worked in the drawing office for 29 years and having a good standard of living and never once said I didn't like my job, because every day was different with the variety of work we had to do. I have great memories of great staff over the years. Thank you all for your kindness shown over the years.

CHAPTER 15

SU AND LOGISTICS MANAGER

Pat Fitzgerald

I commenced working in NET, as it was then, in 1966. I was working in the Sales Office with the late Tom Redmond, Austin and Michael O'Connor. Jimmy Healy and Owen Doyle started working in the office later. NET was a great employer then and up to 1200 worked on the site.

In 1961 the Minister for Industry and Commerce set up a State Sponsored Company, Nitrigin Eireann Teoranta to erect and operate a Nitrogenous Fertilizer Factory at the Shelton Abbey location near Arklow.

There were 1500 people employed by the company at its peak. Hauliers all found work because of NET. Over 2000 tonnes of fertilizer daily were transported from the factory in the busy season. Vehicles from all over Ireland were drawing bulk and bagged loads from the factory.

Much of the bagged fertilizer was also transported by rail from the NET/IFI site in 16/40 tonne wagons. Trains were railed to cork, Tralee, Portlaoise, Derry, Tullamore, Mallow, Ennis, New Ross, Kilkenny, Dundalk and Waterford.

As time went on more and more fertilizer, was transported by road, as Irish Rail could not supply as many wagons as were needed. A lot of bulk nitrogen was exported to Combrie ports, such as Bruges in Belgium, Ayr in Scotland, Itzehoe,in Germany, Bremen and Hamburg in Germany. Nitrogen was also exported ports in the U.K.

EMERGENCY TELEPHONE NUMBERS

SITE..3209

SURGERY 3240

NURSE'S BLEEP...204

FIRST AIDERS (LABORATORY)......................3238

EMERGENCY ASSEMBLY NUMBERS

FRONT GATE..3209

BACK GATE...3537

RECEPTION..3299

LABORATORY...3531

EMERGENCY CONTROL CENTRE...............3532

IRISH FERTILIZER INDUSTRIES ARKLOW SAFETY BOOK

FORWARD

I am pleased to welcome you to Irish Fertilizer Industries and hope you will be happy as a member of our factory staff.

For the safety of all staff it is essential that each person is conscious of the need for exercising care in avoiding accidents.

The most common causes of accidents in our type of industry are,

Handling objects/materials

Stepping on or striking against objects

Use of hand tools

Slips, trips and falls

Burns – steam, hot pipes

Contact with chemicals (liquid or gas)

Burning/welding

Foreign body in eye

These accidents can be prevented if each task is done the safe way, using the right equipment.

The important message of this safety book is that, while the Company will play its part in terms of providing safety training, equipment and procedures, the final responsibility for working safely rests with each individual.

It is essential that you read the book thoroughly, keep it for reference at all times and do your utmost to observe and carry out the precautions set out in it. By so doing you will be helping to play your part in making this factory a safe place to work.

Accidents do not happen – they are caused.

Signed: Bill Flood, Factory Manager 1/1/2000

TABLE OF CONTENTS

SAFETY, HEALTH & ENVIRONMENT POLICY

It is the policy of IFI to manage its activities in accordance with the best practices in the industry regarding Safety, Health and the Environment, to minimize risk to people and property and to reduce impacts on the environment to a practicable minimum. The company supports the principals of sustainable development and therefore is committed to ensuring that its activities do not compromise the ability of future generations to meet their needs.

The application of this policy will be a prime consideration in the management of all IFI activities.

In order to comply with this policy, IFI will:

-Co-operate fully with the relevant authorities in meeting its legal obligations.

-Set demanding targets and measure progress to ensure continuous improvement in S, H & E. performance.

-Require all employees to exercise personal responsibility in preventing harm to themselves, others and the environment.

-Take steps to minimize impact on man or the environment by continuously improving our environmental performance, minimization of wastes at source or re-use and recycle of materials.

-Participate expertly in the discussion of relevant issues with regularity bodies, national/international organizations and industrial/professional associations in order to develop sound S.H & E. policies, practical standards and sustainable practices.

-Use resources with care, having particular regard for those which are scarce and non-renewable. Assess in advance, using the most up-to-date techniques, the S. H & E. implications of any new development or change of existing activity.

-Communicate openly on the nature of our activities and report progress on our S. H. & E. performance.

-Promote the interchange of information and technology between the three IFI factories, promote awareness throughout the organization and provide appropriate training to employees responsible for implementing S.H & E. control measures.

-Promote the aims of the Responsible Care Programme of the – Irish Chemical Industry and adhere fully to its guiding principles.

-Implement, maintain and continuously improve an effective Environment Management System.

<u>RESPONSIBLE CARE</u>

S. H. & E. MANAGEMENT SYSTEM

Policy

The IFI board has adopted a single policy setting down the company position on S. H. & E matters. All employees are required to comply with it.

Standards

The IFI board in conjunction with the Managing Director has also set down S. H. & E. standards (pages 8 - 11) which must be complied with by all company managers. These standards are basic management requirements and compliance with them will enable the realization of the principles of the Responsible Care programme of the Irish Pharmaceutical and Chemical Manufacturers Federation (Republic of Ireland).

Factory Procedures

Each factory shall draw up its own S. H. & E. procedures which set out the arrangements and requirements by which operations are to be carried out in a safe, healthy and environmentally sound way. The factory procedures shall comply with legislative requirements and best practice in the Chemical Industry.

Auditing

Each factory shall have in place a plan for auditing S.H & E. performance. The audit process is a vital step in safeguarding people, property and the environment and in ensuring that continuous improvement takes place. It involves systematic checking and in-depth examination of activities and systems to assess the effectiveness of implementation of company standards and to identify areas of improvement.

Performance Report /Policy Review

The Managing Director will make an annual report to the Board outlining the extent to which the standards are being complied with, identifying areas of major concern and indicating areas, plans and time scales for improvement. This will be based on the audits of the factories and their regular S.H & E. reports. This report will show the Board how the policy is being fulfilled and provide the basis for further decisions

S. H & E. MANAGEMENT SYSTEM

S. H & E. POLICY

POLICY REVIEW…

STANDARDS

AUDITING

PERMANENT

INSTRUCTION

S.H & E Standards

The method by which the following standards are implemented is through the various Permanent Instructions listed on page 16 – 18.

Organisation & Responsibilities

The policy will be implemented via the existing Management structure, where each member of management is responsible for S.H & E. performance of those reporting to him/her in the same way that he/she is responsible for their other activities at work. Management at all levels are responsible for monitoring S.H & E. performance in their areas and for monitoring and training their staff towards achieving a higher level of S. H & E. performance.

The specific responsibilities of all staff shall be set down by each factory in the S.H & E. Statement.

2. Communication & Consultation

Each factory shall establish suitable systems to ensure that relevant information is available to employees, contractors, customers and the public concerning the effects of IFI's materials, products and activities on the safety and health of people and the environment. Relevant information shall be made available throughout the company to facilitate continuous improvement in performance and there shall be consultation and communication with staff to promote to involvement in improvement programmes.

3. Training

Training needs shall be identified and satisfied in each factory to ensure that employees work with proper regard for the safety and health of themselves and others and for environmental protection. Training and validation arrangements shall be regularly reviewed.

4. Material Hazards

Appropriate information shall be maintained to enable all materials used on site or manufactured for sale to be properly handled, stored, transported, used and disposed of. Each factory shall identify and assess the hazards arising from these materials. Also the appropriate limits of workplace exposure to relevant materials shall be established and disseminated.

5. Modifications & Changes

There shall be arrangements to ensure that no modifications compromise S.H & E. performance. Proposals shall be registered and assessed, and modifications shall be authorised. Necessary hazard studies shall be carried out, appropriate design considerations made and all changes properly engineered and recorded.

6. S.H & E. Assurance

All facilities shall be maintained and equipment to ensure continued safe operation, the health of people and the minimum environmental impact. There shall be arrangements to provide for the periodic review of hazards and for routine inspections of plant, equipment and premises. Such reviews shall have regard for process hazards, engineering integrity, containment of materials, fire protection systems and other measures, to ensure fitness for purpose. Appropriate records relating to equipment, plant or facilities and their processes shall be maintained in each factory.

7. Systems of Work

Systems of work shall be drawn up and maintained to ensure the safety and health of people and the protection of the environment. Hazards shall be eliminated or consequent risks reduced as far as is reasonably practicable. Control measures shall be implemented and monitoring programmes arranged to demonstrate safe working conditions and effective control.

8. Safety Case

Each factory is obliged to prepare a Safety Case in compliance with the requirements of the European 96/82/EC. The Safety Case describes the plant, equipment, systems and procedures for the control of major hazards.

9. Emergency Plans

Each factory shall have a formal on-site emergency plan for handling emergences (e.g. injury, fire and explosion, toxic release, environmental damage and security related matters) and arrangements for linking with the off-site plans of the local public services.

10. Contractors & Suppliers

The safety, health and Environmental implications of all aspects of work carried out by others on behalf of IFI shall be considered. There shall be arrangements to ensure that competent contractors are selected, monitored and supplied with sufficient information to ensure that the safety and health of their employees is not at risk of IFI activities. The contractors/suppliers shall be required to provide sufficient information to ensure that the safety and health of IFI employees or others is not put at risk or IFI environmental standards are not compromised. The purchase and supply of raw materials, equipment and services shall be specified and monitored to ensure S.H & E. requirements are met.

11. Environmental Impact Assessment

Each factory shall prepare and maintain an up-to date assessment of the environmental impact of its activities. This assessment shall take into account, but not be limited to solid, liquid and gaseous wastes arising and the measures for their disposal, as well as any land contamination issues and for releases of materials or energy. There shall be arrangements for the proper management and disposal of wastes and for the maintenance of records of all solid, liquid and gaseous wastes generated.

12. Resource Conservation

There shall be arrangements to ensure that natural resources are conserved by efficient energy use and by minimising the consumption of non-renewable resources, the conservation of flora and fauna and the reduction of waste to the minimum practicable. Re-use and recycling of materials shall be promoted, having regard for Safety, Health and Environmental, social and economic factors.

13. Soil and Groundwater Protection

Each factory shall have arrangements to minimise the risk of contamination of land and groundwater and maintain a dossier which records the history and contamination of the site and a register of all leaks and spills which may have potential for land contamination. Each factory shall assess and review at regular intervals possible contamination on its land and the need for protective, containment or remediation measures.

14. Performance & Reporting

Each factory shall have arrangements for reporting safety, health and environmental performance and for investigating and recording accidents, incidents and public complaints and for taking appropriate corrective action to prevent recurrence. Records shall be maintained and information and statistics reported to the Board regularly.

15. Auditing

Formal auditing procedures shall be defined and implemented to ensure that the systems adopted to meet these standards are soundly established, maintained and observed. Deficiencies identified during audits shall be formally recorded and their implications assessed and corrective actions prioritised and acted upon.

STAFF RESPONSIBILITIES FOR HEALTH & SAFETY

Factory Manager

1. The implementation of company S.H & E. Policy at the Arklow factory.

2. The maintenance of the necessary organisation to implement that policy.

3. The monitoring of Factory Operations to ensure that the Policy is being implemented.

4. The establishment of acceptable targets and standards of performance in relation to S.H & E. matters.

5. Ensuring that there are adequate Permanent Instructions (PI's) to control the operations at the factory.

6. Ensure that those responsible to him are properly trained and are competent to carry out the work required.

Operations Manager

1. The implementation of the factory S.H & E. Policy for the Production and Engineering Departments.

2. The safe and proper operation of all plant and equipment.

3. The proper maintenance of all plant and equipment.

4. The systematic implementation of all statutory and internal company registration and inspection.

5. Ensuring that all equipment installed and designed and constructed to acceptable engineering standards.

6. Ensuring that any modifications made to plant or equipment are designed, constructed, tested and maintained to the same standard or better than the original plant or equipment.

7. Ensuring that those responsible to him are properly trained and are competent to carry out the work required.

Fire & Safety Advisor

1. To assist and advise management in the implementation and maintenance of the company S.H & E. Policy.

2. To monitor the implementation of the Policy and report on departures from agreed methods and standards.

3. To Co-ordinate the drawing up of Factory Safety Procedures and Permanent Instructions and to assist management as required.

4. To draw up an Emergency Plan and test the Plan.

5. To monitor all safety aspects of shutdown work and ensure that IFI and contractor employees are adequately briefed on safety matters and working safely.

6. To ensure site safety equipment is serviceable and adequately maintained.

7. To liaise with Local Authorities and Statutory Bodies on fire and safety matters.

8. To provide appropriate safety training courses for site personnel and contractors.

9. To participate in investigation of serious accidents/incidents and monitor remedial action.

Section Managers/Engineers

1. The implementation of Factory S.H & E. Policy in the areas of which they are responsible.

2. The safe and proper operation of plant and associated storage of materials.

3. The establishment and maintenance of a system of plant instructions which specifies the conditions and standards to which a plant must be operated.

4. The regular monitoring of all aspects of operation, work and housekeeping in the area to ensure acceptable standards are met.

5. Ensuring that no changes are made to agreed operating or maintenance standards without agreement of the Department Manager.

6. Ensuring that appropriate safety communication takes place with staff and conducting regular area safety meetings.

7. Ensuring that those responsible to him, including contractors, are properly trained and are competent to safely carry out the work required.

Operations Foremen

1. The implementation of Factory S.H & E. Policy in the area of which they have responsibility.

2. The safe and proper operation of the plant and associated equipment.

3. The implementation of plant instructions, particularly those specifying the conditions and standards to which plant must be operated.

4. The regular monitoring, on a day-to-day basis, of all aspects of operation, work and housekeeping in the area to ensure standards are being met and that problems and potential problems are highlighted quickly.

5. Ensuring that the Permit to Work system is rigidly adhered to.

6. Ensuring that all personnel within their charge are provided with detailed instruction, including safety aspects, of any work they are required to do.

7. Ensuring that no changes are made to plant equipment or operating instructions which are outside accepted limits or previous instructions, without prior consultation with the Plant Manager.

Maintenance Foremen

1. The observance of the Factory S.H & E. Policy in the area for which they have responsibility.

2. Ensure that the Factory Safety Procedures are followed in the area for which they are responsible.

3. Provide adequate instructions on work detail and methods to those in their charge.

4. Ensure that those issuing permits to work are briefed on the nature and extent of the work and to ensure that the conditions specified in the permits to work are fulfilled.

5. On completion of work to ensure that equipment is safe to run, i.e. ensure that all guards are replaced, equipment is appropriately tightened and any debris is removed.

6. Ensure that personnel in their charge are properly equipped to carry out the job.

7. Ensure, on a day-to-day basis, that the equipment for which they are responsible is in good condition and will not cause harm to those in the vicinity.

FACTORY EMPLOYEES

1. (a) To take reasonable care for their own Safety, Health and Welfare, and that of any other person who may be affected by his/her acts or omissions while at work.

(b) To co-operate with his/her employer and any other person to such extent as will enable his/her employer or the other person to comply with any of the relevant statutory provisions.

(c) To use in such manner as to provide the protection intended, any protective equipment or other means provided for securing his/her safety while at work.

(d) To report to his/her immediate supervisor, without unreasonable delay, any defects in plant, equipment or system of work which might endanger safety, health or welfare, of which he/she becomes aware.

2. No person shall intentionally or recklessly interfere with or misuse any appliance, protective clothing, equipment or any other thing for securing the safety, health or welfare of other persons.

Factory Permanent Instruction System

Compliance with the safety standards is achieved by the factory Permanent Instruction System. These instructions cover the full range of activities and operations on site. Compliance with the Factory Permanent Instructions is mandatory and all personnel should be familiar with Instructions relevant to their work. The full list of Permanent Instructions is given below.

A Policy

A1 S.H & E. Policy Document

A2 S.H & E. Improvement Plans

A3 S.H & E. Resources

A5 Provision of Factory S. H & E. Instructions

A7 Management Structure

B Training

B1 Provision of Training in S.H & E. matters

D Safety

D2 Operating and Maintenance Instructions

D3 Plant information

D4 Isolation from fluids

D5 Isolation from Energy Sources

D6 Handover of Work

D7 Permit to Work

D8 Entry into Confined Spaces

D9 Excavations/Break-in

D10 Hot Work

D1 Ignition Sources

D12 Safe Work on Low & Medium Voltage systems

D12A Safe Electrical Work on High Voltage Systems

D 14 Work on Roofs

D 15 Gas detectors

D 16 Work on Unfenced machinery

D 19 Lone & Isolated Workers

D20 Mobile work Platforms

D21 Fork Lift Trucks

D23 Road Vehicles

D25 Decontamination of Equipment

D25A Chemical Cleaning of Equipment

D26 Erection & Inspection of Scaffolds

D26A Control of Ladders

D29 Use of Flexibles and Hoses

D35 Task Assessment

D36 Loading of Tanks/Containers

D36A Guidance for Labelling Road Tankers

D37 Manual Handling

D103 Crack Detection

E Health

E3 visible Display Terminal

E4 Smoking

E7 Hazard Data

E8 Control of Chemical Agents Hazardous to Health

E9 Asbestos

E10 Ionising Radiation

E11 Protection against Noise

E11A Occupational Screening Audiometry

G Personal Protection

G1 Personal Protective Equipment

H Inspection and Maintenance

H7 Piping Systems

H8 Machine Guarding

H10 Alarms, Trips and Interlocks

H16 Programmable Electronic Systems

H100 Control of Compressed Gas Cylinders – Valves

J Technology Controls

J5 Modifications

J6 Modification to Programmable Electronic Systems

J8 Area Classifications

L Purchasing Controls

L1 Use of Contractors' Services

P Accident investigation

P1 Reporting of Accidents etc.

Q Fire & Emergency

Q1 Fire Management

Q2 Emergency Plans

Q 100 Toxic Refuges

PERMIT TO WORK SYSTEM

Under the Safety, Health and Welfare at Work Act 1989, the Employer has a duty to provide and maintain plant and systems of work that are, as far as is reasonably practicable, safe and without risks to health. At IFI Arklow the principal system is the Permit to Work System which is fully described in the Factory Permanent Instruction D7: Permit to Work.

The Permit to Work is essentially a document which is used between the person responsible for process and maintenance. In it are recorded:

- A statement of the agreed work to be done on a given item of plant.

- The condition of the item of plant.

- The potential process hazards associated with the item, and the precautions to be taken.

- Any restrictions to maintenance activities because of the potential interaction between those activities and process.

The issue of a Permit to Work does not:

- Make the job safe.

- Form an instruction for the work to be done.

Only authorised personnel may issue or receive a Permit to Work. All personnel doing work under a permit must be familiar with the Works Permit Instruction D7: Permits to Work. It is important to note that a personal padlock must be fitted on the switch by everybody included on the Permit to Work and the plant or equipment must not be reconnected until all the personal padlocks are removed before the plant/equipment is electrically reconnected. Also, in all cases the people responsible for the plant/machinery must have someone walk around the equipment before it is switched on to be satisfied that nobody has arrived at the equipment unseen. This rule came in after the engineer arrived at a conveyor unknown to the process operators, got inside the conveyor and was killed because the operator switched the equipment on thinking that there was no one in the plant.

ENTRY INTO CONFINED SPACES

NEVER enter a tank, vessel, pit drain, or confined space without an ENTRY PERMIT.

Normally a second person (Standby Person) will be posted at the entrance to vessel as a safety precaution.

The person entering the vessel MUST

- Read and comply with the precautions listed on the Entry Permit.

- Use any protective equipment required.

- Come out of the vessel etc. if he feels the conditions have changed.

THE ROLE OF THE PERSON OUTSIDE THE VESSEL (STANDBY PERSON)

THE PRIMARY ROLE OF THE STANDBY PERSON IS TO SUMMON HELP SHOULD ANYTHING HAPPEN TO PEOPLE IN THE VESSEL AND TO ENSURE THAT ONLY THOSE WHO ARE PERMITTED WILL ENTER THE VESSEL.

In order to fulfil this vital function the following points shall be observed by the Standby Person:

A. The Standby Person shall remain alert and attentive to what is happening inside the vessel. He/she shall keep those inside in sight. If this is not practical, an effective means of communication shall be set up to maintain contact with those inside the vessel. He/she shall listen for voices and noises which might indicate that a problem has arisen.

B. Other than to summon help should an emergency arise the Standby Person is not permitted to leave the entry point of the vessel while anyone is in the vessel.

C. The Standby Person shall enter not enter the vessel to attempt rescue. If anything happens he/she shall summon help by calling the nearest Process Person, or phone, or break glass unit, or radio if he/she has been issued with one.

An Emergency Break Glass Unit may only be used if one is nearby. Use of Emergency Break Glass Unit shall be followed with a phone call. The phone number to dial is 3209 (Emergency phone at Security).

He/she shall familiarise himself/herself with the locations of the nearest phone and break glass unit.

D. When anyone wishes to enter a vessel, no matter who that person is, the Standby Person shall ask him/her if e/she has permission from the Plant Senior Operator (Named Person) and shall get him/her to read and sign the Entry Permit. No one may enter unless he/she has permission from the Senior Operator and has signed and read the permit

E. The Standby Person shall at all times know the exact number of people in the vessel. This is vital in the event of an emergency. It will not be sufficient to know the approximate number. If many people are involved in the entry, names of people shall be written down as they go in and crossed out as they come out.

F. If the Emergency Alarm sounds the Standby person shall call out those in the vessel and stop others going in until the Senior Operator gives them permission to go back.

G. The Standby Person shall inform the Senior Operator when everyone has left the vessel. The Standby Person shall affix a "No Entry" to the entrance of the vessel when everyone has left the vessel.

H. The Standby Person shall ensure he/she understands other requirements set out in the Entry/Work Permits.

I. The Standby Person shall ensure that no person who is unprotected by breathing apparatus approaches close enough to point of entry to put him/herself in danger from the atmosphere in a confined space containing a hostile atmosphere.

TASK ASSESSMENT

Many accidents happen during both routine and no-routine work due to insufficient preparation or thought on the safety aspects of the task at hand. All employees should form the habit of carrying out a mental risk assessment before performing a task or instructing others to do so.

The following guidelines will assist you in carrying out a mental risk assessment.

STOP, THINK then CONSIDER

- Is there a standard instruction/procedure for this risk?

- Have I/they had experience previously of this kind of work?

- Is it a routine or non-routine task?

- Is it a task which might affect other people's work?

- Is it an abnormal stage in an otherwise normal routine?

- What are the hazards associated with the task – are the risks tolerable?

- Has there been adequate preparation and planning?

- How complex is the task?

- What is the level of competence and experience of the person(s) carrying out the work?

- Is the briefing/instruction, supervision and assistance adequate?

If having mentally assessed the job you have no reservations the task may proceed OR If you have a query which you are unable to resolve you must seek assistance from someone who has the appropriate experience, or access to the relevant information. If you are still unable to resolve the problem it shall be referred local Plant/Area Management.

CONTROL OF SUBSTANCES HAZARDOUS TO HEALTH

All substances brought onto site must be assessed under the 1994 Chemical Agents Regulations. The purpose of the assessment is to ensure that the relevant precautions are identified before the substance is used.

Each plant area has its own Handbook containing Hazard Data, Sheets for each hazardous substance used in the area. These sheets are available for inspection and contain details of permitted exposure levels, action to be take in the event of accidental contact. ingestion and any special precautions or control measures that must be taken when handling that substance.

All employers must be aware of the risks to their health from exposure to such substances in their area and the precautions that must be taken.

Employees must also co—operate in personal monitoring checks, make full and proper use of any protective equipment provided, report any defects in that equipment and practice a high standard of personal hygiene.

The following are the main hazardous chemicals with which you may come into contact during the course of your work, or which may affect you in the event of an incident.

MAIN CHEMICALS PRODUCED/USED ON SITE – HAZARDS & PRECAUTIONS

NITRIC ACID

What? A colourless liquid giving off acrid vapours

Where? Nitric acid is produced and stored on the nitric acid plants

It is also transferred by pipeline to the C.A.N. Plants.

Hazards

Nitric acid is a powerful oxidising agent which burns the skin, eye tissues and all mucous membranes. Its vapours are corrosive to the respiratory tract and can cause fluid build-up in the lungs which could prove fatal.

Protective Clothing

Gloves, goggles, safety boots, safety helmet and overalls must be worn at all times when entering pump or storage areas on the Nitric Acid Plants. For any operations where contact with nitric acid is a possibility a PVC acid suit must be worn.

Emergency Treatment

Swallowing – wash out the mouth and give large quantities of water.

Eyes – use eyewash bottle immediately.

Skin – wash with large amounts of water.

AMMONIA

Ammonia is a strong alkali. Ammonia gas has a very strong characteristic smell also known as anhydrous ammonia liquid and liquefied ammonia) is colourless and gives off pungent vapours. Brought in by train, stored in the spheres and transported by pipeline to the Nitric Acid and C.A.N Plants for use.

At very low concentrations ammonia gas causes coughing and may damage or destroy tissue. Higher concentrations could be lethal. Liquid ammonia causes severe burns to the skin and permanent damage to the eyes. If ingested it causes severe damage to the tissues of the mouth and the gastro-intestinal tract.

Protective Clothing

For any operation where contact with ammonia is a possibility use self- contained breathing apparatus and fully protective ammonia resistant suit, hood and boots. For routine operations chemical gloves, goggles, safety boots and safety helmet are

Required.

Emergency Treatment

Inhalation - remove injured person from contaminated area and get medical attention.

Eye Contact - irrigate eyes for at least ten minutes with clean water and get medical attention.

Colourless to yellow liquid

AMMONIUM NITRATE

A white solid. In the C.A.N. Plants a concentrated solution of Ammonium Nitrate is present which is called Ammonium Nitrate Liquor.

Ammonium Nitrate is produced by reacting ammonia and nitric acid on the C. A. N. Plant.

It is an oxidising agent. In its liquid form it will burn the skin on contact.

Protective Equipment

PVC gloves, overalls, safety boots and safety helmet, goggles/light eye protection. For operations where contact with ammonium nitrate liquor is a possibility a PVC suit is required.

Emergency Treatment

Remove from area. Wash with large quantities of water. Get medical help.

SULPHURIC ACID

Sulphuric Acid is a colourless to yellow liquid giving off acrid vapour. It is stored in IFI storage tank at Roadstone. It is transported to site, stored in the site storage tanks and used in the C.A.N. Plant.

It is highly corrosive to all parts of the body. Its vapours are corrosive to the respiratory tract and can cause fluid build-up in the lungs which could prove fatal.

Protective Clothing

Gloves, goggles, safety boots, safety helmet and overalls must be worn when entering pump or storage areas. For any operations where contact with sulphuric acid is a possibility a PVC Acid suit must be worn.

Emergency Treatment

Swallowing - wash out mouth and give large quantities of water.

Eyes - use eye wash bottle immediately.

Skin - wash with large quantities of water.

HYDROCLORIC ACID

Hydrochloric Acid is a colourless or slightly yellow fuming liquid. It is stored in Nitric Acid 5 Demin Plant and used for water treatment.

Its hazard - irritating to eyes, respiratory system and skin.

Protective Clothing

Gloves, goggles, safety boots, safety helmet and overalls must be worn at all times when entering pump or storage areas. For any operations where contact with Hydrochloric Acid is a possibility a P.V.C Acid suit must be worn.

Emergency Treatment

Swallowing - wash out mouth and give large quantities of water.

Eyes - use eyewash bottle immediately.

Skin - wash with large amounts of water.

COUSTIC SODA

In liquid form it is colourless and odourless. In solid form it is white flakes. It is stored and used in Boiler Units 460 and 2700 and in the Nitric Acid Plants for water treatment. Its hazards - it is corrosive (Strong Alkali).

Protective Clothing

Gloves, goggles, safety boots, safety helmet and overalls must be worn at all times when entering pump or storage areas. For any operation where contact with caustic soda liquid is a possibility a PVC Acid suit must be worn.

Emergency Treatment

Swallowing - wash out mouth and give large quantities of water.

Eyes - use eyewash bottle immediately.

Skin - wash with large amounts of water.

PRODUCTION AREAS

1. You MUST be conversant with the nature of the chemicals used on your plant.

2. You MUST protect yourselves and your fellow employees when using chemicals.

3. You MUST get proper medical attention after emergency treatment if you have an accident involving chemicals.

4. You MUST adhere strictly to the correct process procedures and instructions while operating plant and equipment.

PRESSURE VESSELS

1. Before allowing work on Pressure Vessels make sure a Work Permit has been obtained.

2. Before opening any vessel, ensure that the pressure has been released to atmosphere.

3. Ensure that all materials have been removed and all covers, manways and hatches are secure before placing the vessel under pressure.

VALVES AND LINES

1. After opening a valve, leave the handwheel slack and not jammed against the stop.

2. Do not climb over lines to reach a valve. Arrange for a mobile platform or ladder to be used.

3. Do not allow lifting gear to be strung from process piping.

MACHINERY

1. Know your machine, and operate it carefully.

2. Do not remove guards without authorisation.

3. Never wear loose clothing and particularly neck ties around machinery in motion.

4. All machinery must be completely isolated before repair work is commenced - see section on Permit to Work.

5. Never climb over, or insert sticks, bars or shovels, in to moving machinery, particularly conveyers.

6. Always ensure all guards are back in position before starting up machinery.

NET January 21st. - Joe - saved to this PC.

MAINTENANCE WORK

1. NEVER clean or repair machinery whilst it is in motion.

2. NEVER drill material which is not secured or clamped.

3. NEVER remove chips or swarf by hand. Use a rod or brush.

4. NEVER drop gas or oxygen cylinders.

5. NEVER lubricate or use jointing compounds on gas cylinder valves - particular oxygen, which could explode.

6. NEVER fool around with compressed air.

7. NEVER start work without getting a Permit to Work in plant areas.

8. NEVER wear loose clothing when working near moving machinery.

9. NEVER work on roofs or high up without using safety equipment.

10. ALWAYS use guards on machines when provided and wear the correct goggles when grinding, burning or welding.

11. ALWAYS look out for your fellow employees. Use the welding screens, etc., provided.

12. ALWAYS use correct hoses for gases. On gas cutting sets the black is for oxygen and the red is for acetylene. NEVER change over the hoses.

13. ALWAYS replace machinery guards securely after completion of work.

14. ALWAYS tidy up the area after finishing the job.

15. ALWAYS replace manhole covers before you leave the job site.

16. ALWAYS fence off holes in floors, pits, etc., if you have to leave the job.

SCAFFOLDING

The use to which a scaffold is put will determine how substantial it needs to be. Scaffolds should only be designed, erected, altered or dismantled under the direction of a competent person and by competent and experienced workers. Scaffolds should be inspected weekly by a competent person.

Does your scaffold meet the requirements? Check these points as a guide.

1. Adequate foundation - placed on level, firm ground with base plates and sole plates where necessary.

2. Platforms 3 - 5 boards wide, depending on use.

3. Each scaffold board on a working platform with at least three supports - supports not more than 1.5m apart.

4. Scaffold boards either tied down or overhanging each end support by at least 50mm and not more than 150mm.

5. Vertical supports not more than 2 - 2.5.

6. Scaffold braced along the diagonals to stiffen it both along and at right angels to its length.

7. Scaffold tied in to the building at least every 4m vertically and 6m horizontally.

8. Guardrails and toe-boards along the outside edge and at the ends of any working platform from which people or materials could fall more than 2 meters.

9. Toe-boards at least 150mm high with no more than 750mm between the top of the toe-board and the guardrail.

10. Guardrail 1m above the platform.

NET January 21st Joe - saved to this PC

LADDERS

1. Before using a ladder check that it is free of safety defects.

2. All ladders must have a stable footing and be securely fixed at the top or attended by a person at the bottom.

3. Ladders must not be used at an angle of less than 70 degrees to the horizontal - approximately 1 in 4.

4. Access ladders should have an over-reach of 1 metre or suitable hand-holds must be provided.

5. Where ladders are secured vertically to mobile staging, care must be taken to ensure that there is minimum interference between the tubes on the staging and ladder rungs (i.e. there is no obstruction in the way of a person's foot).

6. Two ladders must not be lashed together to form one longer ladder.

7. Ladders must be placed so that the steel reinforcement is at the lower sides of the rungs.

8. Ladders must not be used to support staging.

9. It is a statutory offence to paint ladders in such a way as to cover up defects.

10. Do not try and stretch too far to one side when at the top of a ladder.

11. Have someone foot the bottom of the ladder and make sure that nobody bumps into it. OR, secure the ladder with lashing or footing.

LIFTING TACKLE

1. Lifting tackle must not be used to lift loads over the specified Safe Working Load.

2. Treat all equipment with respect. You may be near when there is a failure.

3. Never stand or pass under suspended loads.

4. Never risk using equipment which looks to be damaged.

5. After use always ensure that lifting equipment is properly cleaned and stored. Prolonged exposure to fertilizers can cause sudden failure.

TOOLS

1. Use the correct tool for the job.

2. Return all defective or damaged tools to the stores. Do not continue to use them.

3. Non-spark tools must be used in flameproof areas and when specified on the Permit to work.

TRIPS AND FALLS

1. Keep walkways, stairs and working areas clean, tidy and dry. Clean up spills immediately.

2. Use the safe route and avoid short cuts.

3. Watch where you are going.

WORK ON ROOFS

Never work on a roof without first obtaining a Permit to Work.

Flat Roof

- Guardrails and toe-boards must be adequately secured and set back from the edge.

- Wear safety harness for edge work.

Sloping Roof

- Wear safety harness.

- Use crawling boards or ladders, secularly fixed.

- Ensure catch barriers are erected at eaves or working platform at least two boards (430mm) wide with guardrails or toe-boards.

Fragile Roof

Roof materials may be made of cement asbestos sheet, glass or plastic which may not be strong enough to support a person's weight.

- Wear safety harness.

- When working on or passing across fragile roof materials use two crawling boards - one to stand on while the other is positioned.

- walking the line of bolts securing sheets is dangerous.

- Use purlin trolley equipment (complete with guardrails) when large quantities of sheets are being placed.

- Valleys, channels or gutters near fragile materials to have guardrails

Or other suitable protection.

Sheets being moved in windy conditions may act as a sail, causing loss of balance.

PERSONAL PROTECTIVE EQUIPMENT

Personal Protective Equipment (PPE) is provided to protect you from injury. People working at IFI Arklow are expected to observe the Site's minimum requirement for Personal Protective Equipment.

SAFETY HELMETS must be worn at all times when working on site.

LIGHT EYE PROTECTION must be worn at all times within plant boundaries/workshops/laboratory.

CHEMICAL GOGGLES and/or FACE SHIELDS must be worn when:-

-Handling acids, caustic soda, ammonia or other hazardous fluids.

- Grinding or chipping.

- Welding or burning.

- When specified on your Work Permit.

SAFETY BOOTS must be worn within plant boundaries, stores and workshops.

GLOVES must be worn where necessary to protect hands. Make sure to use correct type of glove for the task at hand.

DUST MASKS are available should it be necessary to work in dusty conditions.

APRONS and PROTECTIVE SUITS are available when working with hazardous fluids, in wet areas or when such protection is specified in your Work Permit.

SELF CONTAINED BREATHING APPARATUS AND RESPIRATORS ARE AVAILABLE TO PROTECT AGAINST GAS AND FUMES.

SAFETY WITH ELECTRICITY

When you work around electricity:

MAKE SURE all equipment is suitable for the job and properly earthed or insulated.

FOLLOW INSTRUCTIONS use machinery as its designed to be used and work carefully.

REPORT UNSAFE CONDITIONS and any equipment that may have problems.

Safety Rules

1. NEVER interfere with electrical equipment or plant unless so authorised

2. NEVER lay cables across roadways, passages or doors unless they are -

3. NEVER touch anyone who has received an electric shock and who is still in contact with the power source – use a dry coat, dry rope or stick to disconnect them.

4. ALWAYS inform the first aid centre immediately, in the event of a person receiving a shock and if the person is unconscious apply artificial respiration.

5. ALWAYS check that your tools are flameproof if working in flameproof areas.

6. ALWAYS tackle electrical fires with CO_2 or Dry Powder extinguishers. Other types are dangerous.

ELECTRICIANS

- ASSUME ALL LINES ARE LIVE UNTIL YOU PERSONALY HAVE PROVED THE DEAD.

- MAKE SURE THAT NO CIRCUIT CAN POSSIBLY BE MADE LIVE WHILE PEOPLE ARE WORKING ON IT.

1. You must be familiar with the Electricity Regulations, and follow the Permit to Work System.

2. When "LIVE" working is essential, always have an assistant in close attendance.

3. Do not trust rubber insulation gloves alone – BE CAREFUL.

4. Always make certain when performing isolations by pulling fuses or locking off.

5. Do not trust memory – other lives may depend on you.

6. Remember that isolation capacitor banks may retain charge.

7. Make sure the system is completely discharged before starting work.

8. Always short out "DEAD" terminals before starting work.

9. Familiarity breeds contempt – BE CAREFUL.

GENERAL OFFICE SAFETY

1. Do not place obstructions on stairs or gangways. Use handrails when ascending or descending.

2. Do not put cables of telephones, portable electric appliances and office machines where they will trip anyone.

3. Close filing cabinet drawers after use and, to avoid overbalancing the cabinet, have only one drawer open at any one time.

4. Use suitable knives and cutters for paper, board, string, sharpening pencils, and so on.

5. If you have to climb, do not use office chairs, boxes, etc. Use a suitable step stool or step ladder.

6. Do not carry any load too heavy for you and make sure that you can see over the top of any load you are carrying.

7. Keep articles of clothing and any other combustible materials away from heaters. Do not dry wet clothes on space heaters, the build-up of heat will cause a fire.

8. Any spillages must be reported ad immediately wiped clean.

9. Do not obstruct access to fire-fighting equipment, make sure you know how to use the equipment.

10. Before leaving work, switch off all electric appliances.

11. Keep your desk tidy.

12. Report any defective items to your supervisor.

13. Smoking is not permitted in offices.

LABORATORY SAFETY

Improperly handled, many laboratory materials can cause burns, poisoning, sickness, disease, fire or explosion. Follow established procedures when handling them.

KNOW YOUR MATERIALS

Know the physical properties and potential dangers of materials you use in the lab. Consider how they may react in combination. Handle all materials with care.

CHECK CHEMICALS PROPERLY

Don't breathe reagents or other chemicals directly. Never attempt to identify chemicals by smell.

READ LABELS CAREFULLY

All materials should be properly labelled with contents, record of date purchased/opened, expiry date, etc. Follow any special precautions noted. Don't use any unidentified material. Dispose of unlabelled, or outdated chemicals properly.

USE MECHANICAL SUCTION AIDS

Never use your mouth for suction for pipetting hazardous liquids, use a pipette pump.

DISPLAY WARNING SIGNS WHEN HAZARDS EXIST

For example, put up notices when you're using hazardous substances.

CLEAN UP SPILLS IMMEDIATELY

For dry spill; Disinfect if necessary, then wash area of spill and wipe dry.

For wet spills, - Soak up with absorbent material or special "spill kit" then clean up absorbent and wipe area dry. Put waste materials in approved, labelled containers.

ENSURE POPER VENTILLAION

Use fume - or other appropriate devices to remove hazardous gases or fumes, to prevent build-up of combustible vapours or when handling chemicals that give off fumes.

TAKE OTHER PRECAUTIONS

Don't leave experiments or active processes unattended. To prevent fires, don't use flaming or sparking equipment unless you're sure no flammable materials are present. Always check Safety Data Sheets for Highway Code

SMOKING IS PROHIBITED

GOOD HOUSEKEEPING

DO keep your place of work clean and tidy.

DO put you're rubbish in the bins provided.

DO keep doors, gangways and stairs unobstructed.

DO note the position of fire-fighting and BA equipment.

DON'T remove safety guards unless authorised to do so.

DON'T leave material spilled on the floor, sweep or mop it up.

DON'T tamper with fire-fighting or safety equipment – your life may depend on it.

DON'T run in the plant – trips and falls (at ground level) are the most common causes of industrial accidents.

DRIVING ON SITE

Driving on site is conducted under the normal rules of the High Code and is subject to speed limits displayed on road signs (15MPH). Know the limits and observe them.

ALCOHOL/DRUGS

It is forbidden to bring onto, or to consume alcohol/drugs on this Site. If in the opinion of a representative of management, an employee is considered to be under the influence of drink/drugs, then that employee will not be allowed or continue work.

SMOKING

Smoking is forbidden at all times except when in designated smoking areas.

MANUAL LIFTING

When lifting heavy articles-

(a) Get a good grip of the article.

(b) Keep your back straight.

(c) bend your knees.

(d)lift steadily and firmly. Do not jerk.

(e)make sure you are wearing your safety footwear.

2. Get assistance if the article is too heavy for you.

MANUAL HANDLING

1. Use gloves when handling rough materials.

2. Watch out for the other person.

3. With drums and casks, be sure that they cannot run away either when stacked or whilst handling.

4. Watch out for excess in drums when attempting to open them – using the correct key.

5. Wear protective equipment when handling hazardous substances.

NOISE, AN UNNSEEN HAZARD

The European Communities (Exposure to Noise) Regulations, 1989 require that the Company operates systems to prevent damage to employees' hearing caused by noise at work. Sound level readings have been taken across all plant areas and as a result some areas have been designated mandatory or advisory ear protection areas.

- When sound levels exceed 83db(A) the use of ear protection is mandatory. Areas above 83db(A) are signposted by hearing protection signs. You will be issued with a plan showing noise levels on each plant.

Additionally you are expected to:

- Wear approved hearing protection when required to by the Permit to Work system.

- Ensure that any device (e.g. silencers) fitted to any equipment in order to noise is properly fitted before you use it.

- Report to your foreman any defect in noise reduction equipment, e.g. acoustic lagging, ear protection equipment, or any significant increase in noise levels that you notice.

- Only approved types of hearing protection should be used.

FIRE & SAFETY EQUIPMENT

Fire Extinguishers

There are two types of extinguishers in use on site;

CO2 – coloured red with black label/band. Suitable for most fires including flammable liquids or electrical apparatus.

Dry Powder - coloured red with blue label/band. Suitable for most fires including flammable liquids and electrical apparatus.

Make sure you know where the nearest fire extinguishers are and how to use them.

Always ensure that used fire extinguishers are returned to the stores for refilling.

Fire Water Hose Reels /Fire Hydrants

Are placed Strategically around the site and in plant areas.

WATER MUST NOT BE USED ON LIVE ELECTRICAL EQUIPMENT OR FLAMMABLE LIQUIDS.

SELF CONTAINED BREATHING APPARATUS

There are two types of self-contained breathing apparatus strategically placed in process plants.

- Standard 35-minute SCBA sets – must only be used by trained personnel.

20-minute SCBA sets – must only be used by trained personnel.

There are also full face mask cannister respirators and emergency escape filter respirators strategically placed in process plants. Make sure you know how to use them.

NEVER INTERFERE WITH ANY SAFETY APPARATUS – ONE DAY YOUR LIFE MAY DEPEND ON IT

FIRE PRECAUTIONS/PREVENTION

1. Smoking is forbidden except when in designated smoking areas.

2. Rags and oily waste must be put in the bins provided.

3. Do not leave wood or combustible material near pipelines for steam, nitric acid or ammonium nitrate.

4. Report leaks or spills of any process fluids.

5. Never carry out hot work without first obtaining a Hot Work Permit.

BASIC INGREDIENCE OF A FIRE

AIR   HEAT

(Smoother it)   (Cool it…)

FUEL

(Starve it)

TAKE ONE INGREDIENT AWAY AND THE FIRE STOPS!

OCCUPATIONAL HEALTH DEPARTMENT

Occupational health is concerned with the relationship between

Health and work. It studies both the effect of health on the ability to work and the health problems that work can cause. The role of the site Occupational Health Department is to prevent or minimise adverse effects of work on employees' health and to advise whether persons are fit for their work.

Health Promotion

- Developing an awareness of health risks and educating employees so that they can keep themselves fit to be at work.

Health Assessments

- All employees are required to undergo a health assessment prior to commencing employment with the company.

- Health assessments are required annually and at other times during employment, for example after illness or accident.

Medical Services

- Treatment of work-related illness or injury.

- Advice on any effect on health thought to be work related.

- Investigation into any problems related to health at work.

HYGIENE

- Keep your messroom clean and tidy.

- Wash your hands before eating and after you have been handling chemicals, or have been in the toilet.

- Use barrier cream on your hands before starting work if needed.

- Use the protective clothing and equipment provided.

- Use after care cream at end of working shift if needed.

FIRST AID

1. The Works Medical Unit is for **YOUR** benefit.

2. Always get treatment no matter how slight the injury.

3. Get initial treatment from an experienced First Aider.

4. An injured person must not be moved until proper attention has been given unless there is a threat of further injury from fire, toxic or corrosive materials. ,

5. If an injured person seems lifeless give artificial respiration immediately. Prompt action can save lives.

6. If splashed, wash the affected parts immediately with large amounts of clean water. If eyes are affected use eyewash bottle.

7. An oxygen resuscitator is available in the First Aid Room.

ACCIDENTS/INCIDENT REPORTING PROCEDURES

1. All accidents, incidents or unexpected happenings must be reported to your supervisor as soon as possible.

2. The prime reason for the report is to PREVENT a RECURRANCE – NOT to lay blame. Your co-operation towards this aim is essential.

3. YOUR help is needed to keep the factory safe and in good repair.

- Report any missing safety equipment.

- Report any equipment in need of repair.

4. Suggestions for improving the safety of any job, equipment or plant should be discussed with your supervisor or by using the SAFETY SUGGESTION SCHEME.

A SAFE WAY THROUGH THE CHEMICAL I NDUSTRY

After many years in the Chemical Industry our advice to any new Starter is to be your own safety officer. As with any other job to become your own safety officer you must serve an apprenticeship

- Whichever plant or workshop area you are to work in make sure that you know the inherent dangers.

- Listen to your Foreman and fellow employees when they describe possible hazards.

- Safety equipment is always available – make sure you use it.

- Fire and anti-gas drills are carried out regularly – make sure you know what to do in an emergency.

- As well as the site alarms – know what your plant /area alarms mean.

- Always wear the appropriate safety gear.

- Always keep your work area tidy.

- **THE RULES AND PRECAUTIONS IN THIS BOOK ARE NECESSARY** FOR YOUR OWN SAFETY. Never be complacent, don't take short cuts and above all, BE SAFE – BE YOUR OWN SAFETY OFFICER

Joe Weadick Fire & Safety Advisor 1/1/2000

COMPANY DOCTOR & COMPANY NURSES

Our company doctor from the start of the factory 1965 to 1993 was Dr Declan Connolly of the Richard King Medical Centre 3 Upper Main Street, Arklow.

From 1993 to the close of the factory was Dr Ian Bothwell of Arklow Medical Practice, 3 Upper Main Street, Arklow. They were both excellent doctors and were always ready to do any medical work on our staff requested by management.

From the start to the closure of the factory we had a full-time nurse in our First Aid/Medical room. The nurses who worked in that important job were, Nurse Mary Whitty, Nurse Betty Kavanagh, Nurse Esther Murray, Nurse Mary O'Donaghue, Nurse Jean Carty and Nurse Ann O'Shoughnessy.

Xray Facilities

For the first five years the factory had to have employee xray's carried out by a mobile Xray unit hired in every year. It was then decided to have our own Xray unit built at the east end of the Laboratory which was operated by NET Nurses.

CHAPTER 16

THE DEMISE OF IFI

Joe Weadick

In the Irish Parliament debate in February 1999, Ms. Harney, the minister for Enterprise, Trade and Employment, made it clear that she was anxious to test the market with a view to securing a purchaser with a commitment to IFI as a fertilizer manufacturer and who was prepared to give safeguards regarding IFI's operations and its level of employment. She repeated at a later stage that employment maximization would certainly be the first priority.

There was considerable speculation about the amount of money which the sale of IFI would realize. In 1998 there were reports in the press that the State hoped to benefit from the sale of IFI based on estimates which valued the company at around 100 million. A government sources statement that these estimates were very wide of the mark was followed by a later report in the Irish Times (16th September 1999) that the sale was likely to make 50 million. Minister Harney further stated in the debate in the Irish Parliament in February 1999, that there must be a reasonable return to the exchequer since all of this has cost close to 400 million since the early 1980's. It became apparent that the State wanted to do better than 51 per cent of the sale proceeds and had reached agreement with ICI on the State share of the return.

Throughout 1998 and the first half of 1999 there were reports of two bidders for the purchase of IFI. One was from a Galway based company, Grande Portage, and the other was a joint approach from IAWS and Kemira, the latter a Finnish International chemical group with an Irish base in Hillsborough, Northern Ireland. In May 1999 the Irish Times reported that the sale of IFI might be shelved because it had failed to reach ICI's reserve on it.

The Irish Government still appeared at this stage to be putting greater emphasis on the preservation of the jobs of IFI's existing workforce.

Between May 1999 and March 2002 there was little evidence of efforts to sell IFI. At this stage approval was given to progress negotiations for a possible merger between IFI and Kemira's UK operation. It was subsequently learned that in August 2002 contact had been made with a number of companies with a view to selling IFI but of these only four expressed any degree of interest. It was concluded, therefore, that the production of ammonia would be shut down at Cork, and Kemira would supply Arklow and Belfast with ammonia. Failure to reach agreement with Kemira and a breakdown in these negotiations was announced by RTE on 10th of September 2002.

After this the events moved rapidly. IFI's revised business plan for 2002/3 showed that the company could not achieve break-even in the coming year. This plan depended on support from the employees as well as a share-holders loan of 10 million to avoid a cashflow problem. The shareholders in their response were of the opinion that the revised plan was not viable as it was vulnerable to unforeseen shocks and that the loan of 10 million in that event might not prove adequate. In these circumstances the request for the loan was denied.

113

In the light of this impossible situation the directors of IFI decided on a Liquidator to the company and that the liquidation of the company should proceed on the basis of members' voluntary liquidation so that disengagement from the industry can proceed in an orderly manner. The shareholders were unable to support this request and consequently a creditors voluntary liquidation was initiated. **This took immediate effect on 15th of October 2002 when the shutdown of all the company's plants at Cork, Arklow and Belfast began and was followed by the inevitable dismissal of the company's employees.**

With the appointment of a liquidator, fertilizers stocks were sold and the dismantling of a number of plant items begun following their sale to buyers in various parts of the world. No buyer was found who was prepared to acquire IFI as a company with the intention of operating all or some of its plants to produce fertilizers. This meant that the decision of the directors on 15th October 2002, to recommend the appointment of a liquidator, heralded the end of the fertilizer manufacturing in Ireland.

There will be those who will argue that IFI's position was untenable because of external factors including the high cost of fertilizer prices and the uncertain demand for fertilizers. Others will claim that IFI's excessive capital expenditure programme had a serious effect on their financial position and will lay the responsibility for this at the feet of the management and the board of directors. There will be those critics who will point to the lack of strategic vision of the shareholders who jointly formed IFI in 1987 and by 1998 seeking to disengage from the fertilizer industry. In particular the change in commitment of the majority shareholder, the Irish Government, to the fertilizer industry demonstrated a volte-face.

In 1965 the Irish Government entered the fertilizer industry through the formation of a state-owned company, NET, and the building a nitrogen fertilizer plant in Arklow. The rational for this state-owned enterprise derived from the importance of fertilizers as an input to Irish agriculture and the strategic position of agriculture in the Irish economy.

By 1998, when the Irish Government had expressed its intention to withdraw from the industry, their primary concern, as expressed by the minister Ms. Harney, was now the preservation of the IFI employee's jobs. Finally, in October 2002 RTE reported that the minister, Ms. Harney, in commenting on the liquidation of IFI, said that although IFI was the only producer of fertilizers in the country, there was no shortage of supplies for the Irish market and added that it was no longer the strategic industry it had been in the past.

The strategic importance of the industry in the past has been well documented. In two world wars the industry made a major contribution to feeding the nation at a time when imports of foodstuffs were severely restricted. Perhaps we are now conditioned by recent events to the belief that wars will last only two or three weeks and that isolation for an Island people is no longer a real threat to food security. In such a case we can more readily accept that the **fertilizer** industry like each of other major industries such as shipbuilding, textiles, synthetic fibers and garment manufacture has a natural life cycle. and that what we have witnessed with the demise of IFI is the end of the fertilizer manufacturing industry's life cycle in Ireland. But the issue of food security will always be with us, and its importance, though apparently diminished, should not, nevertheless be underestimated. **A question must remain, therefore, whether it is prudent strategically for an Island such as Ireland to be completely devoid of the capacity to produce this key input to the food chain.**

I do not believe for one minute that major industries like fertilizer manufacture, ship building, textiles manufacture, synthetic fibers and garments manufacture have a natural life cycle.

We knew for years that the Kinsale natural gas would have heated every home in the country if it was not used for making ammonia. In 1998 the government should have put pressure on the IFI directors to search for and agree with some European or middle east company to supply ammonia to Arklow and Belfast on a long-term contract, similar to what prevailed for years before Marino Point was built. Then close down Marino Point and give the workers there the entitlement of five weeks for every years-service. We, in Arklow, were actually making money when the company was liquidated. I will never forget the injustice done to us.

Joe Weadick, Safety Advisor in the Arklow Plant

NET 12th of April 2024 – Joe - saved to this PC.